THE ONCE AND FUTURE KING

T. H. White

D0887358

SPARK PUBLISHING

SPARKNOTES is a registered trademark of SparkNotes LLC

Spark Publishing
A Division of Barnes & Noble
120 Fifth Avenue
New York, NY 10011
www.sparknotes.com

ISBN-13: 978-1-4114-0725-1
ISBN-10: 1-4114-0725-3

Please submit changes or report errors to www.sparknotes.com/errors.

Printed in the United States

10 9 8 7 6 5 4 3 2 1

CONTENTS

CONTEXT

TERENCE HANBURY WHITE WAS BORN in 1906 in Bombay, India, to British parents. He was educated at Cheltenham College in England and Queen's College in Cambridge, where he graduated at the top of his class. White led a solitary life, and other than his few friends from the academic and literary world, his only companions were his pets. White was particularly heartbroken when his dog Brownie, a red setter, died after fourteen years of faithful friendship. White did make one attempt to get married, but his heart was not in it and his would-be fiancée eventually broke off their relationship. Toward the end of his life, White underwent psychological treatment for homosexuality. White was also an on-again, off-again alcoholic, and though his drinking never ruined him, it was enough of a problem that he made repeated, unsuccessful attempts to stop drinking entirely.

Early in life, White taught at several English preparatory schools. His first successful book was an autobiography called *England Have My Bones*. He was eventually able to make enough money from his novels, particularly from the four books that make up *The Once and Future King*, to dedicate himself to writing full time. In his spare time, White was a passionate falconer, pilot, sailor, goose-hunter, fisherman, and scholar of medieval texts. It was in this last capacity that he began studying the Arthurian legends, stories about the legendary King Arthur that date as far back as the early twelfth century and have become an integral part of British literature. White's own interpretation of King Arthur would become the subject of his best-known novels.

Although *The Once and Future King* was White's best-selling novel, three of the four books that make up the completed work were first published independently: *The Sword in the Stone* in 1938; *The Witch in the Wood*, later renamed *The Queen of Air and Darkness*, in 1939; and *The Ill-Made Knight* in 1940. The fourth book, *The Candle in the Wind*, first appeared in 1958, when it was published in the completed *The Once and Future King*. White also wrote a fifth book, *The Book of Merlyn*, in which Merlyn and Arthur discuss the issue of war, using the animals that Arthur had known as a child, but it was rejected by White's publisher. That book has since been published but has never been considered equal to White's classic novel. In the years since its initial publication, *The Once and Future King* has enjoyed a popularity that spreads far beyond bookstores. White's novel is the basis for the classic Lerner and Lowe musical *Camelot*, which debuted in 1960, and for the animated Disney film *The Sword in the Stone,* which premiered around the time of White's death. White died in Athens, Greece, in 1964, at the age of fifty-seven.

PLOT OVERVIEW

IN BOOK I, "The Sword and the Stone," we are introduced to the Wart, a young boy who eventually becomes King Arthur. The Wart grows up in the castle of Sir Ector, his foster father. The Wart spends his days in the company of Kay, Sir Ector's son and the heir to his title, amusing himself as best he can while Kay is instructed in the proper ways of knighthood. One night while lost in the forest, the Wart encounters the magician Merlyn, a befuddled but powerful old man who announces that he will be the Wart's tutor. During the next six years, Merlyn tries to instill some of his wisdom in the Wart, teaching him about virtue and the world by turning the Wart into various animals. Finally, Kay is knighted, and the Wart becomes his squire, a kind of servant who assists and attends to his master as the knight travels in search of adventure. When the king of England, Uther Pendragon, dies, he leaves no heir, and it is proclaimed that the next rightful king will be whoever can pull out a mysterious sword that has been driven into a rock. The Wart and Kay travel to London, where a tournament is being held so that the finest knights will have the opportunity to try to remove the sword. While running an errand for Kay, the Wart removes the sword from the stone, and he is declared the next king of England.

Book II, "The Queen of Air and Darkness," finds the young King Arthur, as the Wart is now called, trying to hold on to his power. Of the men rebelling against Arthur, his most notable enemy is King Lot of Orkney. As the war rages on in England, Lot's sons, Gawaine, Gaheris, Gareth, and Agravaine, compete for the affections of their mother, the beautiful but cruel Morgause. By a twist of fate, Morgause is also Arthur's half-sister, though he does not know it. Three knights from Arthur's court arrive at Orkney, and unaware that their king is at war with Lot, they proceed to bumble around the countryside. Although Gawaine, Gaheris, and Gareth are all decent at heart, they and their brother, Agravaine, are happiest when they are listening to stories about their proud heritage and dreaming about wars and bloody revenge.

In England, Arthur begins to plan how he will rule when the battles are finally over. With Merlyn's guidance, he decides to use his own power and that of his fellow knights to fight for people who cannot defend themselves. Arthur creates an order of knights to fight for good, called the Knights of the Round Table. Then, with the help of two French kings, Bors and Ban, Arthur defeats Lot's army at the battle of Bedegraine. With her four children, Morgause travels to Arthur's court, supposedly to reconcile Arthur with Lot. While at the court, she uses magic to seduce Arthur. Arthur is not aware that Morgause is his half-sister, but the incest is still a great sin, and by sleeping with her, Arthur ultimately brings about his own destruction.

Book III, "The Ill-Made Knight," focuses on the great knight Lancelot and his moral conflicts. Lancelot is just a boy when King Arthur takes the throne, but he eventually becomes Arthur's greatest knight and best friend. Trying to escape his growing feelings for Queen Guenever, Lancelot embarks on a series of quests that establish his reputation. In the last of these, he is tricked into sleeping with a young girl named Elaine. Guenever grows increasingly jealous of Elaine, and her jealousy eventually drives Lancelot insane. He roams England for several years as a wild man, unrecognized and ill-treated by everyone he meets. Finally, Elaine discovers Lancelot and nurses him back to health. Although Lancelot does not want to feel obligated to Elaine, he does, and on two occasions he leaves Camelot to spend time with her and their son, Galahad. Meanwhile, Arthur's kingdom begins to unravel, and he tries to keep his knights occupied by sending them to find the Holy Grail. Only three knights, Sir Bors, Sir Percival, and Sir Galahad, are pure enough to find the holy vessel. Lancelot returns a humbled and deeply religious man. For a while, his love for God makes him stay away from Guenever, but after he rescues her from a kidnapper, they begin their affair again.

In Book IV, "The Candle in the Wind," the destruction of Camelot becomes inevitable. Mordred, Arthur's son by his incestuous union with Morgause, plots revenge against his father. Mordred and Agravaine trap Arthur into acknowledging the affair between Lancelot and Guenever, which forces Arthur to prosecute his queen and his best friend. Lancelot rescues Guenever from being burned at the stake, but in doing so, he kills two of Gawaine's brothers, Gareth and Gaheris. Arthur and his armies lay siege to Lancelot's castle. The pope sends an emissary to broker a truce, and Guenever returns to Arthur's castle at Camelot. Arthur and Gawaine, however, still want to avenge the deaths of Gareth and Gaheris, and they continue to besiege Lancelot. While they are away, Mordred usurps the throne. Arthur rushes back to reclaim his kingdom. The night before his final stand against Mordred, Arthur reflects on all he has learned since his youth and wakes up confident that although this day will be his last, his legacy will live on.

CHARACTER LIST

King Arthur The protagonist of the novel. Arthur is known as the Wart in the first book and as King Arthur once he is crowned. He is a conscientious, slightly timid young boy who becomes king of England after being tutored by Merlyn. Arthur believes in justice and in doing what is right, but his faith in good sometimes makes him blind to the intrigue around him.

Lancelot Arthur's best knight and the commander of his forces. Lancelot has a love affair with Guenever, Arthur's queen. Lancelot is a deeply conflicted figure. Although he is considered to be the greatest knight in Arthur's court, he struggles constantly with feelings of guilt and inadequacy. He is doggedly faithful to those who love him, even if they do not always have his best interests at heart.

Merlyn A magician who has already lived the future, so he knows what is going to happen next. Merlyn is Arthur's tutor and friend. Arthur's creation of the Round Table and a more civilized England is largely due to Merlyn's influence. Although Merlyn is powerful, he is also kind and a little absentminded.

Guenever Arthur's wife and Lancelot's lover. Guenever is beautiful, jealous, and often petty. She is, however, a fundamentally decent person. She understands and supports Arthur's ideas and loves Lancelot despite his great ugliness.

Mordred The son of Arthur and his half-sister, Morgause. Cold, calculating, and vicious, Mordred is raised by Morgause to hate Arthur. He thrives on slander and insinuation, which he prefers to open confrontation.

Morgause The mother of Gawaine, Gaheris, Gareth, and Agravaine, and the half-sister of Arthur. Morgause is cruel and petty, but her little whims have a huge impact on Arthur and England. Her seduction of Arthur is the first step in Arthur's destruction.

Elaine A girl Lancelot is tricked into sleeping with, and the mother of Galahad. Although still very young, Elaine is crafty and determined enough to do all she can to win Lancelot's love. Except for the two times she persuades Lancelot to stay with her, Elaine is an unhappy woman, well aware that Lancelot loves Guenever.

Galahad Lancelot and Elaine's son. Galahad is morally perfect and invincible and the only knight holy enough to find the Holy Grail. He is so perfect, in fact, that he often seems more like an angel than a human. Galahad is disliked by all but a few of Arthur's other knights.

Gareth Morgause's sweetest and most sensitive son. Unlike most of his brothers, Gareth loves Arthur and Lancelot.

Gawaine Morgause's oldest and strongest son. Gawaine, prone to murderous rages, is in many ways an emblem of everything that is wrong with knighthood. Despite Gawaine's roughness, however, he is a decent man.

King Pellinore The first knight Arthur meets. An amiable bumbler whose lifelong quest is to hunt the Questing Beast, Pellinore becomes an accomplished knight after his marriage. Even after Pellinore is killed, his legacy of kindness lives on in his children.

Sir Kay Arthur's foster brother and a knight of the Round Table. Spoiled as a child, Kay remains nasty and selfish, but is decent at heart.

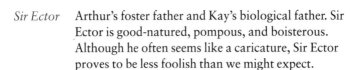

Sir Ector   Arthur's foster father and Kay's biological father. Sir Ector is good-natured, pompous, and boisterous. Although he often seems like a caricature, Sir Ector proves to be less foolish than we might expect.

The Questing Beast   A magical creature that only a Pellinore can hunt. The Questing Beast needs to be hunted to survive, and after a series of comic mishaps, it is hunted by Sir Palomides instead of King Pellinore.

Agravaine   One of Morgause's sons. Agravaine seems to have the most problems with his mother's promiscuity. As a child, Agravaine is the cruelest of Morgause's sons, and he remains deceitful and cowardly throughout the novel. He is Mordred's closest ally.

Sir Bruce Sans Pitié   An evil knight known for his sneak attacks and ambushes. Sir Bruce always manages to avoid capture and is a recurring example of the old injustices that Arthur is trying to fight.

Uncle Dap   Lancelot's childhood instructor. Although he is the brother of kings, Uncle Dap is Lancelot's squire when Lancelot becomes a knight of the Round Table.

Morgan le Fay   Morgause's sister and Arthur's half-sister. Morgan le Fay, who is most likely a fairy queen, shows up periodically to torment knights and villagers with her malicious spells.

Nimue   Merlyn's lover, who eventually traps him in a cave for centuries. Despite her faults, Nimue is basically a nice woman, and she promises to take care of Arthur on Merlyn's behalf.

Sir Thomas Malory   In the novel, a page whom Arthur asks to carry on the Arthurian ideals of justice. In real life, Sir Thomas Malory wrote the fifteenth-century text *Le Morte d'Arthur,* an account of the Arthurian legends that served as the basis for White's novel.

Uther Pendragon The king of England during Arthur's childhood. Uther Pendragon is actually Arthur's father. Once Pendragon dies, the next king is determined by a trial, which Arthur wins. Thus, Arthur is eventually placed on the throne after Pendragon's death.

ANALYSIS OF MAJOR CHARACTERS

KING ARTHUR

King Arthur is the protagonist of *The Once and Future King* and the novel's narrative and emotional center. The novel follows Arthur's life from beginning to end, and the major events in his life shape the story. After Arthur becomes king, his ideas about government reshape English society, and these changes determine the plot, chronology, and setting of the four books that make up the novel. Even the novel's title promises that although the story ends with Arthur's death, he will always be England's ruler. Despite Arthur's extraordinary importance to the novel, however, he is a fairly simple character. As a child, Arthur (then called the Wart) is honest, trusting, modest, and good-hearted, and he preserves these qualities when he becomes king. King Arthur shapes his government with an important new philosophy that makes him a great king, but the ideas are Merlyn's rather than Arthur's. Arthur is exceptional because he believes in these ideas and is able to enact them when he becomes king.

Arthur develops a sense of world-weariness and wisdom in the novel's later books, but this development is gradual and his basic nature is not drastically altered. Benevolent optimism keeps Arthur from acknowledging Lancelot and Guenever's love affair early in the novel; later, the same benevolence causes him to persuade them to keep their behavior secret. Even as he grows older and wiser, Arthur is incapable of acting harshly toward the people he loves, no matter how hurtfully they treat him. In a sense, it is Arthur's very simplicity and earnestness that enables the downfall of his reign. While the direct cause of the tragedy is Arthur's incestuous affair with Morgause, we do get a sense that Camelot is also doomed because it has stagnated. The energy and progress of Arthur's early reign slows to a halt, and Arthur becomes a defender of the status quo. This lack of innovation sets in around the time that Nimue imprisons Merlyn, suggesting that Arthur cannot think and develop without his old tutor. It is as though Arthur can only ride the momentum of his earlier ideas without forming any new ones. As Camelot stagnates and the quest for the Holy Grail takes its toll on the Knights of the Round Table, the Orkney faction is able to gain more power, until Camelot is too corrupt to survive.

LANCELOT

Lancelot is the protagonist of Book III and the greatest knight in the company of the Round Table. He is Arthur's best friend and a powerful foil for the king since he is complex and full of contradictions. Lancelot is also Arthur's opposite in that, while he is always able to take swift and decisive action, he is rarely able to use this ability to make the world a better place. Even when Lancelot performs a heroic deed, he does so accidentally, not because he has heroic ideals or good intentions. Lancelot's ugliness gives him a sense of unworthiness and inadequacy from a very young age, but this low self-esteem is paired with an astonishing, almost unnatural talent for all knightly skills and endeavors. The ease with which Lancelot wins glory as a knight, combined with his gnawing sense of inferiority, is the source of most of his contradictions. Lancelot is both religious and lustful, both hideous and exalted, both meek and violent. He is simultaneously Arthur's best friend and betrayer.

Lancelot is a prisoner of such contradictions. His own complexity keeps him from growing as a person, since he is too humble to exalt in his success and allow it to improve his self-image. Cutting through all of these contradictions is Lancelot's unyielding, passionate love for Guenever; ultimately, their affair becomes both the best and the worst thing to happen to him. Lancelot's love for Guenever provides Lancelot with moments of bliss but also compounds his guilt and leads to his downfall.

GUENEVER

Queen Guenever is the third figure in the love triangle that dominates the novel's second half. She is also the least developed of the novel's central triad, which is consistent with White's tendency to focus on male characters. White often stereotypically describes women as being girlish or needy, like Elaine, or as cruel vamps, like Morgause. Unlike Arthur and Lancelot, Guenever does not seem to have any particularly remarkable qualities that mark her as a great or noteworthy queen. She is beautiful, but she is also jealous, selfish, petty, and shallow. Guenever is capable of love, and she loves Arthur as genuinely as she loves Lancelot, though not as passionately. While Lancelot's guilt about their affair reaches epic proportions and threatens to destroy him, any guilt Guenever feels is secondary to her constant craving to be with Lancelot. She even handles their cover-up badly, and at one point she is visibly excited to be reunited with Lancelot even in front of Arthur. As Guenever ages, she tries desperately to stay young and beautiful, as her pathetic attempts to cover her flaws with too much makeup demonstrate. In the novel's third book, "The Ill-Made Knight," White writes that it is "difficult to imagine" Guenever, and this difficulty translates to her role in the novel. She is a central character, but she is important more for the way others feel about her than for anything she herself does or feels.

THEMES, MOTIFS & SYMBOLS

THEMES

Themes are the fundamental and often universal ideas explored in a literary work.

THE RELATIONSHIP BETWEEN FORCE AND JUSTICE

One of White's most radical departures from previous versions of the King Arthur legend is the way he describes Arthur's character. Previous versions of the story, including Sir Thomas Malory's, tend to glorify Arthur as a great hero in conventional terms of military glory and valorous deeds, but White presents Arthur as a political innovator. White implies that Arthur is a great king not because of his strength on the battlefield, but because of his success at translating Merlyn's morals into a just system of governance.

White's main interest in this area, which he shows throughout the novel, is the relationship between strength and justice, which Arthur calls might and right. The medieval England of Arthur's youth is unable to distinguish between might and right, and strength becomes its own justification. Whatever might does is considered to be right in this society. White's negative view of this attitude is evident in his biting satire of medieval knights in the early chapters of the novel. From the Wart's early experiences with the warlike ants, the peaceful geese, the power-hungry pike, and the wise badger, he learns alternatives to the notion that might equals right. Arthur then tries to institute these alternative ideas throughout England. White implies that modern and progressive civilizations are based on the idea of using force to create and maintain a just political system. Arthur is successful because he creates a more civilized England. Eventually, however, Arthur's hard work is undone by internal tensions and by Mordred's treachery. This turn of events suggests that as long as justice depends on force, it will face obstacles and setbacks.

THE ROLE OF WAR IN MEDIEVAL ENGLAND

Arthur's England, particularly during the early part of his reign, is dominated by various forces competing for political prominence.

Therefore, war is inevitable, and war emerges as one of the major themes of *The Once and Future King*. But White presents war as an inexcusable barbarism, a pointless and ugly tragedy. Merlyn tells Arthur that the only time the use of force is justified is for self-defense.

The novel maintains an antiwar stance partly to challenge the important role that war plays in the rest of the Arthurian canon. Unlike in other classic Arthurian texts, the battle scenes in White's novel are few and not terribly graphic. In the few battle that are in the novel, White satirizes knighthood and emphasizes the bloodshed and carnage that necessarily accompanies war. White underscores this point with the lessons that the Wart learns during his tutelage. In the Wart's adventures in the animal kingdom among the fish, ants, and geese, he develops a sense that war is essentially unnatural. The only animals that practice war as a matter of course are the ants, and they seem more like robots than living beings. By the time Arthur becomes king, he has begun to understand how to see through the myths that glorify war and to understand the injustice of using might to make right. For instance, at the beginning of "The Queen of Air and Darkness," the novel's second book, Arthur realizes that knights on a battlefield are essentially bullies, hiding in suits of heavy armor as they slaughter the defenseless and innocent.

THE FRIVOLITY OF KNIGHTHOOD

The engine of war in Arthur's England is kept operational by knights, the legendary soldiers of the Middle Ages. The knights are the might half of the might-versus-right conundrum that Arthur is trying to solve, and they serve as protectors of Camelot's moral codes. Nonetheless, because knights rely on muscle instead of morals, the novel examines them in much the same way it examines war. White often depicts knights as oafish clowns, in contrast to their portrayal as heroes and romantic figures in earlier interpretations of the King Arthur legend.

White also illustrates the tension between the brutal violence of knightly behavior and the elaborate codes of morality and courtesy that knights must follow to maintain their honor. This hidden tension between violence and chivalry is best embodied in the figure of Lancelot. He seems to be an almost unrealistic character, as he encounters so much death and violence without ever losing his commitment to honor. However, we know that emotionally, Lancelot is more insecure and uncertain about his honor than any other knight.

White's more humanized portrayal of knights undermines our ideas about the mythical warriors and warns us against idealizing them. These men cannot live up to the expectations of being both strong knights and pious men, and as a result, Camelot and the order of knighthood break down.

MOTIFS

Motifs are recurring structures, contrasts, and literary devices that can help to develop and inform the text's major themes.

MYTHS AND LEGENDS

The Once and Future King relies heavily on a variety of myths and legends to tell its story. Most notably, the entire novel is a reworking of the Arthur myth. White continually acknowledges that he is modernizing old stories by referring specifically to his sources. For example, the novel contains many asides about Sir Thomas Malory, quoting passages and pieces of dialogue from his fifteenth-century *Le Morte d'Arthur.* Malory even appears as a young page at the end of the novel. White flips the Arthurian legend around by constantly calling attention to the fact that his story has a precedent and by then exposing that precedent's flaws. At times, it seems as if White is interested in debunking the validity of knighthood and also attacking the myths and legends that have romanticized knighthood for so long.

BLOOD SPORTS

White expresses the conflict between the brutality and courtesy of knighthood by making frequent reference to blood sports, such as hunting and hawking. Like knightly warfare, blood sports are motivated by aggression and involve a great deal of brutality. But, like the code of chivalry, blood sports also involve a great deal of tradition and ritual. The Wart's studying, for example, of the "etiquette of hunting" shows that blood sports are governed by a code of etiquette as strict as the one imposed on the bloody business of jousting. Like warfare, therefore, the blood sports in the novel boast a civilized veneer that masks their violent underpinnings.

CASTLES

Each of the different books in *The Once and Future King* revolves around a select few settings, and each of these settings is represented by a single castle that has a unique character. In "The Sword and the Stone," for example, Arthur's home is represented by Sir Ector's

Castle of the Forest Sauvage, a cozy place with a seemingly endless number of nooks and crannies for us to explore along with the Wart. Sir Ector's castle is markedly different, however, from the glorious Camelot or the gloomy castle at Orkney. The castles in the novel have their own personalities that embody the hopes and fears of their inhabitants. Their heavily fortified walls vividly illustrate the separation between the novel's worlds. When Uncle Dap finds Lancelot after his madness, for example, he refuses to enter Castle Bliant. He sits outside its wall, waiting to take Lancelot back to the intrigue of Camelot and Guenever and to leave behind the relatively banal world in which Elaine lives.

SYMBOLS

Symbols are objects, characters, figures, and colors used to represent abstract ideas or concepts.

THE ROUND TABLE

Arthur conceives of the Round Table in "The Queen of Air and Darkness" around the same time that he has his epiphany about might and right. Throughout the rest of the novel, the Round Table is a physical manifestation of Arthur's sense of fairness and justice. The table is designed so that the king's knights will not squabble over rank—there is no head of the table for the best knight to claim as his own. Arthur does not want to create conflicts among knights because he wants them unified in their struggle to maintain peace in England. Even though Arthur's knights show a wide variety of temperaments and frequently scatter across the country, the Round Table holds them together and gives them the name for their order. Therefore, the Round Table is a vital part of Arthur's attempts to subjugate force to justice. It is the focal point of Arthur's war for justice—by not allowing any one knight to gain status over any other, it comes to symbolize the very concepts it has been created to defend.

THE QUESTING BEAST

The Questing Beast represents the absurdity of knightly quests and serves as White's way to deflate the notion of the quest as the route to knightly glory. King Pellinore has no real reason for wanting to catch the Questing Beast—which is not a threat to anyone—and yet he dedicates his entire youth to the project. Remarkably, none of the other knights ever thinks to question Pellinore's dedication, and in their minds, as in his, the quest gives him a purpose. If Pellinore caught the Questing Beast, he would lose the activity that gives his life meaning, and when he has the chance to kill it, he chooses to help the beast instead. Once Pellinore finds real purpose in his love for his beloved wife, however, he forgets about the beast, reinforcing the idea that the Questing Beast is not meaningful in itself but is rather merely something to keep Pellinore occupied.

THE HOLY GRAIL

The Holy Grail, a copper cup or platter used by Jesus at the Last Supper, represents an otherworldly power that even Arthur's knights are incapable of achieving. To find the Grail requires, in addition to knightly prowess, a purity of mind and soul that seems almost contradictory to the ideals of chivalry. The Holy Grail, therefore, symbolizes all that Arthur has not achieved. This revelation that Arthur's England is far from a state of grace also marks the beginning of the end of his reign.

SYMBOLS

SUMMARY & ANALYSIS

BOOK I: "THE SWORD AND THE STONE," CHAPTERS 1–4

SUMMARY: CHAPTER 1

In medieval England, Sir Ector raises two young boys—his son, Kay, and an adopted orphan named Art, who has come to be known as the Wart. The boys are taught chivalry and mathematics, and although Kay makes mistakes in his lessons, he is rarely disciplined, since he will one day inherit his father's lands and title. Drinking port one day, Sir Ector and his friend Sir Grummore Grummursum decide that they should go on a quest to find a new tutor for the boys, since their previous tutor has gone insane. It is July, however, and Sir Ector is busy supervising his tenants while they put the year's hay out to dry. One day after working in the fields, Kay and the Wart go hawking. They take the hawk Cully from the Mews—the room where the hawks are kept—and head into the fields. Even though the Wart is better at handling Cully, Kay insists on carrying the hawk, and he releases him prematurely in the hopes that the hawk will catch a nearby rabbit. Cully, who is in a temperamental mood, flies into a nearby tree instead and perches there, glaring evilly at the two boys.

SUMMARY: CHAPTER 2

Cully flies deeper and deeper into the forest. The Wart worries that Cully's caretaker, Hob, will be disappointed to see so much of his hard work gone to waste, but Kay says that Hob is just a servant, and he storms off. The Wart, however, decides to stay behind and recapture the bird. As darkness falls, the Wart settles down under the tree where Cully has perched. A man shoots an arrow at the Wart, and the Wart runs farther into the forest, losing his way. In the forest, he runs into a knight named King Pellinore. King Pellinore is a kindly, bespectacled man who is on a hunt for a magical creature known as the Questing Beast. The Wart invites Pellinore back to Sir Ector's castle, hoping that Pellinore knows the way or will at least protect him. Pellinore seems tempted, but he suddenly hears the Questing Beast and runs off in hot pursuit, leaving the Wart behind.

SUMMARY: CHAPTER 3

The Wart eventually falls asleep in the dark forest. In the morning, he discovers a cottage and an old man drawing water from a well. The old man introduces himself as Merlyn. He has a long white beard and is dressed in a pointed cap and a gown with embroidered stars and strange signs. He invites the Wart, whose name he already knows, into the cottage, which is full of magical items, strange artifacts, and a talking owl named Archimedes. Merlyn tells the Wart that he is a magician who lives backward in time and that he will be the Wart's new tutor. They leave for Sir Ector's castle, and the Wart marvels that he must have just been on a quest.

SUMMARY: CHAPTER 4

The Wart and Merlyn make their way to the castle, stopping only to catch Cully. When they arrive, Merlyn demonstrates his magical powers to Sir Ector, who dismisses them as sleights of hand, but hires Merlyn nonetheless. Kay belittles the Wart's adventure. Merlyn, who has become suddenly terrifying, chastises him in the formal English of the time. This reprimand makes everybody feel uncomfortable, and Merlyn feels bad for his hot temper. He apologizes to Kay and gives him a silver hunting knife.

ANALYSIS: CHAPTERS 1–4

To fully understand *The Once and Future King*, it is necessary to immerse ourselves in the story's fairy-tale world; White enables us to do so by having his narrator drop in helpful background details and history. We can deduce the personalities of the Wart, Merlyn, Sir Ector, Kay, and King Pellinore from their actions and conversations, but we need to be told everything else explicitly. Bits of history and small details, such as what wine Sir Ector and Sir Grummore are drinking when they converse, are given. The narrative remains seamless, and the novel never feels more like a history book than a work of fiction. White takes great liberties, nonetheless, in telling us all he thinks we need to know. He does not want us to stumble or to only partially understand the story's time period.

To some readers, the story that White is telling is very familiar, since it is a retelling of the traditional tales of medieval England with a modern touch. White's novel is part of the Arthurian tradition, a canon of stories and myths about a legendary Briton king that date back at least to early twelfth-century Britain and France. Although the legend of King Arthur has numerous contemporary interpreters,

White is one of the few to give it modern touches, and he does so to great effect. His story is full of castles, knights, magicians, and serfs, but these characters have desires and speech that are familiar to us. Nowhere is this aspect of the novel better illustrated than in the drunken conversation between Sir Ector and Sir Grummore. While both men are medieval knights, they speak the dialogue of the post-World War I British aristocracy. Fundamentally good-natured, Sir Ector and Sir Grummore are also a pompous pair, and seeing them hem and haw while they drink port makes them more familiar and accessible. By making the two medieval knights sound and act like modern British aristocrats, White makes them more understandable than they would be if they spoke in the language of the time. The characters' uncomfortable reaction to Merlyn's use of formal and outdated language when chastising Kay further demonstrates their modern character.

The early interactions between Kay and the Wart set the stage for our understanding of the boys as they grow, and White makes sure we can empathize with them. The first few chapters are peppered with incidents that help us get an understanding of these two complicated characters. Kay, after losing Cully, angrily states that Hob is only a servant whose feelings are irrelevant, and then he storms off. Wart, on the other hand, spends the night in the forest to find Hob's bird. The Wart seems very much like the good-natured, marginalized stepchild so common in English literature, always decent and eager to please. It is interesting that the Wart is not particularly courageous or full of bravado; rather, he simply does what needs to be done to set things right no matter how frightened he is. Kay, on the other hand, is less pleasant. His actions reveal that he is a spoiled and angry child, so used to having his own superiority asserted for him that he cannot stand to have it challenged. However, he also seems to be a victim of circumstance, since he constantly veers between the haughtiness that his title requires and his own kind heart. He belittles the Wart only when the Wart earns too much praise. Kay's selfish delight in the hunting knife that Merlyn gives him is a touching reminder that Kay's behavior is typical among children his age.

BOOK I: "THE SWORD IN THE STONE," CHAPTERS 5–9

SUMMARY: CHAPTER 5

> *Power is of the individual mind, but the mind's power*
> *is not enough. Power of the body decides everything in*
> *the end, and only Might is Right.*
>
> (See QUOTATIONS, *p. 71*)

Sir Ector's castle is located in the middle of a wild English forest called the Forest Sauvage. On a hot summer day in August, the Wart meets his new tutor, Merlyn, for his first lesson. They stand on a bridge above the castle's moat, and the Wart wishes aloud that he were a fish. Merlyn transforms the Wart into a fish and accompanies him in the moat in the form of a large, wise-looking tench. At the behest of a roach—another, weaker kind of fish—they visit a family of fish whose matriarch is ill, and although Merlyn thinks she is making up her illness, he cures her all the same. Merlyn, who wants the Wart to learn about the dangers of absolute monarchy, brings him to visit the king of the moat, an enormous pike. The pike, who looks a little like Uncle Sam, lazily answers some of the Wart's questions, affirming that power and might are the only two things worth living by. The pike then tries to eat the Wart, but the Wart swims away in the nick of time and is promptly changed back into a boy by Merlyn.

SUMMARY: CHAPTER 6

Kay and the Wart go hunting for rabbits. After Kay kills one rabbit, the Wart fires an arrow into the air. A gore-crow catches the arrow in the air and flies off with it. Kay solemnly pronounces to his angry companion that the bird must have been a witch.

SUMMARY: CHAPTER 7

One day while a sergeant at arms teaches Kay to joust, the Wart mentions to Merlyn that he would also like to be a knight, though he sadly remembers that he is destined to be Kay's squire, an unknighted assistant charged with escorting and aiding knights on their quests. Although Merlyn seems to know that the Wart's gloomy prediction is inaccurate, he keeps this knowledge to himself and says he will allow the Wart to see some real knights. The Wart eagerly picks King Pellinore, to whom he has become attached, and he is magically transported to a clearing in the Forest Sauvage, where he sees

Sir Grummore Grummursum challenging Pellinore to a joust. The two knights engage in a cordial moment and then decide to joust, calling out insults to each other in the more formal high tongue. The battle is a silly one. Each knight is so weighed down by his armor that neither can hurt the other. The two knights charge at each other twice on horses and then a few more times on foot before missing each other entirely and crashing into trees. Merlyn tells the Wart that when the knights wake up, they will be friends. Merlyn then transports the Wart back to the practice ground at Sir Ector's castle.

SUMMARY: CHAPTER 8

Growing bored, the Wart wanders around the castle. Merlyn turns the Wart into a merlin, a kind of hunting bird, and puts the Wart in the Mews with the other birds for the night. There, the peregrine falcon, the bird in charge, asks the Wart about his ancestry and challenges the Wart to prove himself. As a new member of the group, he must show himself worthy by perching within reach of Cully, the goshawk, until the other hawks have rung their bells three times. Cully, who is so used to killing, attacks the Wart, who barely escapes as the bells ring for a third time. In song, the birds hail him as "the King of Merlins."

SUMMARY: CHAPTER 9

The next morning, the Wart wakes up in his own bed, and Kay accuses him of violating curfew the night before. The Wart refuses to tell Kay about the previous night, and the two begin to fight. The Wart receives a black eye, and Kay's nose begins to bleed. As Kay waits for the blood to stop, he begins to cry because Merlyn has not given him any of the adventures he has given the Wart. When the Wart asks Merlyn why he ignores Kay, Merlyn replies with a parable. In Merlyn's story, the Rabbi Jachanan and the prophet Elijah are given shelter by two men, one kind and one cruel. The kind man's cow dies, and Elijah helps the cruel man fix a wall in his house. When the rabbi asks Elijah why neither man has gotten what he deserved, Elijah replies that if the one man had not been kind, he would have suffered much worse, and that if the other man had not been cruel, he would have fared much better. The Wart continues to demand an adventure for Kay. Merlyn finally relents and tells the Wart that Kay will have an adventure.

ANALYSIS: CHAPTERS 5–9

Each of the magical adventures that Merlyn gives the Wart seems designed to impart a carefully calculated lesson or set of lessons. The Wart learns two important lessons from his transformation into a perch and his adventure in the moat. First, Merlyn's compassion toward the roach shows the Wart that even the meekest creatures deserve help, no matter how silly their ailments seem. Even more important, however, is the Wart's encounter with the old pike who runs the moat. The old pike is the epitome of absolute might, and this portrait of power is unflattering. When the old and evil king pike lunges for the Wart, his many rows of teeth represent the sharp and cruel nature that necessarily accompanies absolute power. It is relevant that White likens the fish, with its lean, smooth jaws, to Uncle Sam, the iconic image of the government in the United States. Written in the late 1930s, while new superpower nations were emerging, *The Once and Future King* explores parallels between the Arthurian world and the modern one and frequently tries to link its morals to contemporary events.

During the Wart's time in the Mews, he sees the murderous insanity of a military society. The birds all place a high premium on the importance of lineage and ancestry, and they refer to each other with military titles. Cully, who has been driven to the point of psychotic behavior, is referred to as Colonel, but even his military discipline cannot prevent him from acting on his murderous tendencies. The Wart demonstrates his courage in the Mews, but his success at the task that the birds force him to complete seems to be a hollow victory, and even being triumphantly hailed as "the King of Merlins" is undermined by the ridiculous trial he is forced to endure.

White renders the battle between King Pellinore and Sir Grummore Grummursum ridiculous, using it to poke fun at traditional notions of knighthood. The fight is relatively pointless, since the knights turn a cordial conversation into a joust simply to satisfy the requirements of their social station. There is also humor in the way the fight unfolds, since each man is so heavily padded that he is barely able to hurt the other or even see well enough to avoid running into a tree. The fact that both Pellinore and Sir Grummore address each other in the most formal medieval English is also humorous and allows White to mock the formal address that is traditionally found in Arthurian tales. Knighthood and battling play an important part in *The Once and Future King*, both for the good and the bad, but in this first chapter they are cast as little more than good-natured buffoonery.

These chapters also foreshadow both a bright future for the Wart and a great evil to come. When the Wart gloomily predicts his life as a squire, Merlyn turns away with a knowing smile. The fact that Merlyn teaches only the Wart tells us that the Wart is somehow special. Clearly, the Wart is bound for something greater than squirehood, but the novel gives no way of knowing that the Wart will become the legendary King Arthur. We learn in the novel's first paragraph that Wart is a nickname for Art, which in turn is short for a longer name, most likely Arthur. No other allusions are given to the Wart's true identity, and these moments of foreshadowing are our only signs that something important is on its way. The crow's catching of the Wart's arrow, however, indicates that the Wart's future may also contain dark elements. Kay's somber statement that the crow is a witch suggests that black magic may soon arrive to counter Merlyn's spells; the bird's capture of the Wart's arrow suggests that the omen foretells of malice for the Wart.

BOOK I: "THE SWORD IN THE STONE," CHAPTERS 10–13

SUMMARY: CHAPTER 10

The Wart and Kay walk toward the Forest Sauvage alongside the strip of barley in Sir Ector's fields. Eventually, they encounter a seven-foot-tall giant named Little John. Little John leads them to the camp of a man he calls Robin Wood, known to the villagers as Robin Hood. At the camp they meet Robin and his love, Maid Marian. Robin tells them that one of his men, Friar Tuck, has been kidnapped by Morgan le Fay, a woman of uncertain origin who is believed to be the queen of fairies. Le Fay has also captured one of Sir Ector's servants, Dog Boy, and a local idiot named Wat. The Wart and Kay agree to help rescue the three men.

SUMMARY: CHAPTER 11

Robin tells the Wart and Kay that although his men will help them get to Morgan le Fay's castle, only innocent children may enter, so the Wart and Kay will have to go on alone. Robin gives the boys a small knife, which he explains will protect them because fairies are afraid of iron. Robin warns them not to eat anything while they are in the castle, since they will be trapped there forever if they do so.

As he gives them his instructions, his men drift in silently for their meal.

That night, the company regroups near the castle, and Marian, Kay, and the Wart successfully sneak past a fierce griffin, a creature with the head of a falcon, the body of a lion, and the tail of a snake. The fairies, hoping to lure in children, have made their castle out of butter, cheese, and meat, but the Wart and Kay find it nauseating. Inside the castle, the Wart and Kay find Morgan le Fay resting on a bed of lard, and Dog Boy, Friar Tuck, and Wat tied to pillars of pork. The boys rescue the prisoners by threatening Morgan le Fay with their knives.

SUMMARY: CHAPTER 12

Although the castle disappears when Morgan le Fay is defeated, the griffin remains and attacks Kay and the Wart as they escape. Robin's men try unsuccessfully to fight the griffin off with their bows. As the griffin leaps toward the Wart, Kay shoots an arrow into its eye, and it dies. The griffin falls on the Wart, breaking his collarbone. Robin's men present Kay with the griffin's head. As his reward for the adventure, the Wart asks only to be able to bring Wat back to Merlyn to see if the magician can cure Wat, who is mad. Back at Sir Ector's castle, the boys are congratulated for their adventure, and Kay is very proud.

SUMMARY: CHAPTER 13

The Wart becomes bored with recuperating from a broken collarbone and asks Merlyn to change him into an ant in one of the colonies Merlyn keeps in a glass tank. Merlyn agrees and tells the Wart to place a reed between the two nests. He then changes the Wart into an ant, and the Wart finds himself at the outskirts of one of the two nests. A sign above the entrance to the colony reads, EVERYTHING NOT FORBIDDEN IS COMPULSORY. In his head, the Wart can hear repetitive broadcasts that alternate between giving orders and directions and playing repetitive, soothing gibberish. The Wart comes across an ant who is busy arranging the corpses of two dead ants. Because the Wart is doing nothing, the ant thinks he is insane and reports him to the central command. Sarcastically, the Wart says he has merely hit his head and forgotten his identity, and the ant finds work for him. As the Wart works, he hears more and more broadcasts that prepare the nest for war with illogical arguments and religious sermons that advocate violence. Just as the two ant colonies are about to go to war, Merlyn returns the Wart to human form.

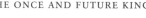

ANALYSIS: CHAPTERS 10–13

"The Sword in the Stone" is often considered to be more directed toward children than the other three books of *The Once and Future King*, and Kay's quest supports this claim. Kay's and the Wart's adventures in the Forest Sauvage are comical, enjoyable, and filled with the typical traits of a fairy tale or a children's story: castles, griffins, fairies, and, of course, the character of Robin Hood. White's principle inspiration for *The Once and Future King* was Sir Thomas Malory's Morte d'Arthur, a fifteenth-century prose rendition of the Arthurian legend that has become one of its most definitive interpretations. In his novel, however, White drastically departs from the characters of Malory's creation. The episode feels like it is a lighthearted jaunt outside of the novel's regular world that tries to delight a younger audience by combining famous characters like Robin Hood with fairy-tale elements like Morgan le Fay and the griffin.

As Kay develops as a character, he remains overly proud and arrogant, but also becomes more likable. We feel more sympathy for the Wart, but once Kay is given his chance to shine, he shows some admirable traits. For example, Kay proves to be very brave, and he has an unerring skill at archery that allows him to shoot the griffin and save his companions. Kay is bound to emerge as the quest's hero, since it is his adventure, but he behaves with courage and good grace nonetheless. The Wart is not a hero in this episode in the same sense as Kay, since he does not win fights or kill beasts. The Wart does, however, have an unusually strong sense of kindness and compassion, and he is consistently selfless. After he and Kay rescue Robin Hood's friends from the fairy, the Wart seeks only to have Wat cured. He is not interested in the superficial trappings of glory; rather, he cares about his fellow human beings and wants what is in their best interests.

The Wart's trip to the ant colony makes a powerful statement on how societies run the risk of becoming overly rigid and uniform. The ant society is clearly communal, but not because each member chooses to work for the common good. Rather, each ant blindly does whatever task it has been assigned. Chillingly, the ants depend on this conformity, and while the Wart is horrified by this cold and faceless society, the other ants find the monotony comforting. Whereas the king pike of the moat demonstrates to the Wart the cruelty of individual tyranny, the ants are an example of the tyranny of the masses, under which freedom is willfully surrendered. This is a society so practical that, as the sign on the tunnels that lead to the gates says, EVERYTHING NOT FORBIDDEN IS COMPULSORY. The emphasis on labor and the contradictory messages that are continuously broadcast have a contemporary ring. The ant society seems to represent communist societies, which often revolved around the idea that each member would labor for the common good. This episode aims not only to teach the Wart how dangerous these supposed utopias can be, but also to alert us to the fallacies of socialist society.

BOOK I: "THE SWORD IN THE STONE," CHAPTERS 14–19

SUMMARY & ANALYSIS

SUMMARY: CHAPTER 14
In November, Sir Ector receives a letter from Uther Pendragon, the king of England, telling him that the royal huntsman, William Twyti, will be coming to hunt near Sir Ector's castle that winter. Sir Ector is expected to house Twyti, his dogs, and his men.

SUMMARY: CHAPTER 15
On Christmas night, the whole village comes to the great hall of the castle to feast. William Twyti is there with his men. The castle and its fields are beautiful under the snow, and everyone is in a good mood.

SUMMARY: CHAPTER 16
Early the next morning, Twyti gathers his men and his dogs for the hunt. With the help of Robin Wood, they find a boar. The boar eventually rushes at Twyti, but Robin kills it with a sword before it can harm Twyti. After the hunt, Pellinore finds the Questing Beast lying sick on the ground and deduces that the beast's decline is his fault. Pellinore is guilt-ridden by the thought that he has been resting in Sir Grummore's castle for months while the beast has pined away in his absence. He gathers men to bring the Questing Beast back to Sir Ector's castle, where he plans to nurse it back to health so the quest can begin again.

SUMMARY: CHAPTER 17
One day in spring, Merlyn, the Wart, and Merlyn's talking owl, Archimedes, have a conversation. The Wart claims that the rook is his favorite bird because it flies as though it has a sense of humor. Archimedes says his favorite bird is the pigeon. Merlyn speculates that the calls of birds and animals are imitations of sounds in nature.

SUMMARY: CHAPTER 18

That night, Merlyn transforms the Wart into an owl. Archimedes teaches him to fly gracefully. Once the Wart knows how to fly, Merlyn turns him into a goose and transports him to a vast, wet plain. The Wart flies with other geese, looks for food, stands guard as they eat, and meets a female goose named Lyo-lyok. She makes fun of his strange behavior, and the Wart tells her that he is really a human. He shocks her by wondering out loud whether they are guarding against an attack by other geese. Lyo-lyok tells him that the idea of two groups of the same species killing each other is unthinkable, since there are already predators outside of their species and since there are no boundaries or territories in the air that can be fought over.

SUMMARY: CHAPTER 19

The Wart learns about the geese's society from Lyo-lyok. The geese have no private property or laws, and their leaders are selected on the basis of their ability to navigate. Soon the time for migration comes, and on their first day of flight, they travel to Norway. The Wart wakes up in his human form to hear Kay, with whom the Wart shares a bed, telling him he snores like a goose.

ANALYSIS: CHAPTERS 14–19

King Pellinore's discovery of the sick Questing Beast in this section satirizes the futility of the knightly quest and makes such quests seem endearing. Hunting the Questing Beast is not only Pellinore's mission in life, but also the mission of his entire family. His discovery of the sick beast, however, demonstrates that he does not really desire to accomplish this goal. Rather than kill the beast and bring the Pellinore dynasty to its final triumph, Pellinore nurses the beast back to health so the chase can continue. In doing so, Pellinore seems to be a somewhat ridiculous figure, more interested in the sense of purpose that the quest brings to his life than in actually accomplishing this purpose. It is hard, however, to fault him for his tenderness toward the creature. As silly as it is for him to keep on hunting when he could finally end his mission, it would be heartless for him to slay the ailing, heartbroken beast. It is interesting too that the bumbling Pellinore, usually so shy and maladjusted, seizes control of the situation here and becomes an assertive, almost admirable figure. This episode suggests that Pellinore's quest is foolish but that he is somehow noble in pursuing it.

The boar hunt is significant because the narrative returns to Kay's quest, during which the novel's morals and philosophy are set aside in favor of a more traditional adventure tale. The boar hunt is an opportunity for White to portray genuine medieval life and has none of the fantastic elements that populate the rest of the story. The animals do not talk, there are no fairies, and neither griffins nor crows threaten Kay or the Wart. This hunt is described in realistic terms and inspires strong emotions. Twyti cries over the death of one of his hunting dogs, and his sadness is believable. This death has more emotional impact than the violence during the Wart's fantastic and surreal adventures. Much like White himself, Twyti lives for his dogs, whose company he clearly values above that of humans; the death of his beloved hound is as heart-wrenching for him as the death of any of his hunters. By taking us outside of the novel's fantasy world, the boar hunt reminds us that there is life outside of Sir Ector's lands and that the land is ruled by a real king.

The Wart's adventure with the geese presents him with a model of society that is nearly the opposite of the one he experiences during his visit to the ant colony. Like the ants, the geese are communal, since they share all property and work, but they elect their leaders, and their communal life does not threaten individual expression. When the Wart mentions the idea of a war among geese, the idea is so foreign to them that it takes a while for Lyo-lyok even to understand what he means. Whereas we can interpret the ant colony as White's attack on the repression of communist societies, the geese espouse a sort of democratic socialism, in which a group of individuals all act in one another's best interests. The novel does not draw any explicit conclusions from these examples but simply presents how they function and what results. Like the Wart, we are expected to draw our own conclusions about which society seems the best and most practical.

Book I: "The Sword in the Stone," Chapters 20–24

Summary: Chapter 20

Six years pass. Kay becomes more temperamental, insisting on using weapons he cannot handle and challenging everybody to fights in which he is invariably defeated. He begins to spend less time with the Wart, since the Wart will soon be beneath Kay's social station,

though it seems Kay is behaving in this way against his will. The Wart is resigned to his fate as Kay's squire.

SUMMARY: CHAPTER 21

Merlyn tells the sulking Wart that the best thing for sadness is to learn something new. Merlyn tells the Wart that this is the last time he will be able to turn him into an animal, since they will soon part ways. Merlyn then turns the Wart into a badger and sends him to visit a wise badger. The Wart, however, in his foul mood, wanders away from the badger's lair and comes across a hedgehog, whom he threatens to eat.

The Wart eventually returns to the badger's lair and talks to the badger, who tells the Wart a story about how man got dominion over the animals. In the beginning, all animals looked like shapeless embryos. God offered to alter each of them in three different ways. The animals chose things like claws for digging and large teeth for cutting. Man was the last embryo to choose, and he chose to stay just as God made him. God therefore gave him dominion over the animals and the ability to use any tool he wanted. The badger wonders, however, whether man has turned his dominion into a kind of tyranny.

SUMMARY: CHAPTER 22

When King Pellinore arrives for Kay's knighting, he brings important news: King Uther Pendragon has died without an heir. A sword, which has been stuck all the way through an iron anvil and into a stone underneath it, has appeared in front of a church in London. On the sword are inscribed the words, "Whoso Pulleth Out This Sword of this Stone and Anvil, is Rightwise King Born of All England." A tournament has been proclaimed for New Year's Day so that men from all over England can come to try to pull out the sword. Kay convinces Sir Ector, Sir Grummore, and Sir Pellinore that they should go to the tournament. While they are talking, the Wart and Merlyn enter and Merlyn announces that he is leaving.

SUMMARY: CHAPTER 23

On the day of the tournament, Kay is so excited that he makes the group get up early and go to the jousting area an hour before the jousts begin. When he arrives, Kay realizes that he has left his sword at the inn, so he haughtily sends the Wart to go back and get it. The inn is closed, however, when the Wart gets there. In front of a nearby church, he sees a sword stuck in a stone. He makes two unsuccessful attempts to pull out the sword. There is a sudden stirring in the churchyard, and the Wart sees a congregation of his old animal friends. With their encouragement, the Wart pulls the sword from the stone with ease. The Wart brings the sword back to Kay. Kay recognizes it as the sword that will determine the next king of England and falsely claims that he was the one who pulled it out of the stone. When Sir Ector presses Kay, however, Kay admits that the Wart pulled it out. To the Wart's horror, his beloved foster father and brother both kneel before him, and he tearfully wishes he had never found the sword.

SUMMARY: CHAPTER 24

The Wart is accepted as king after repeatedly putting the sword into the anvil and drawing it back out again. He receives gifts from all over England. One day, Merlyn appears magically before him. He tells the Wart that the Wart's father was Uther Pendragon and that Merlyn was the one who first brought the Wart to Sir Ector's castle as an infant. Merlyn tells the Wart that from now on he will be known as King Arthur.

ANALYSIS: CHAPTERS 20–24

The Wart's encounter with the hedgehog is the first time that the Wart, in any form, is stronger or more powerful than anybody else, and he has his first experience of tyranny in this episode. Until now, it has always been in the Wart's best interests to disagree with the concept of absolute power, since he is always one of the weakest beings in his world, whether he is a hawk, fish, goose, or human. Now that the Wart is finally in a position to bully somebody, he seems to be on the verge of indulging the same habits against which Merlyn has tried to warn him. When he first encounters the little hedgehog, the Wart is not at all hungry, but his general chagrin at Kay's attitude and Merlyn's departure causes him to threaten the little hedgehog with immediate death. Eventually, however, the Wart's innate sense of decency takes over, and he agrees not to eat the hedgehog. The episode is played for laughs—the hedgehog's pathetic whines are quite ridiculous—and White does not try to draw too much of a moral out of this precursor to the chapter's main encounter. Nonetheless, this encounter reveals the corrupting effect that absolute power can have on even the most well-meaning individuals. The fact that Arthur is able to resist the lure of power bodes well for the many people Arthur soon comes to rule.

The Wart learns a few more valuable lessons during his conversations with the badger. As the badger relates his parable about how man came to dominate the animal kingdom, he also relates the importance of being content with what one has instead of coveting the abilities or position of others. This is an important lesson for the Wart, who is terribly dejected by the thought that Kay will become a knight while he will have to remain a squire. The badger also notes, however, that humanity has not handled its responsibilities well, and he hints that even unexpected gifts should be handled with caution. The freedom to do anything—the kind of freedom that a king of England has—must be accompanied by a sense of responsibility to do the right thing. The Wart learns that to be a good leader he must make ethical, rational decisions that benefit the greater good of his people. Like the other lessons Wart learns from his adventures, these lessons do not seem to have anything to do with his life right now, but they become important when the Wart unexpectedly becomes king.

The events in the narrative of the final chapters occur quickly. The story jumps ahead six years; Kay is knighted, King Uther dies, Merlyn leaves, and the Wart pulls the sword out of the stone and becomes the next king. The previous chapters move at an almost methodical pace, paying attention to many seemingly trivial conversations and events. It is surprising, therefore, that the plot moves at such speed in the final chapters, as these chapters include such important events as Kay's knighting and Arthur's coronation. The rapid pace, however, reflects how sudden and unexpected the Wart's coming to the throne is. The fact that so much changes so quickly also seems to indicate that Arthur's becoming king of England will mean huge changes not just for Arthur, but for the country as well.

Book II: "The Queen of Air and Darkness," Chapters 1–5

Summary: Chapter 1

In an uncomfortable castle in Orkney, a medieval kingdom in Ireland, four brothers, Gawaine, Gaheris, Gareth, and Agravaine, whisper to one another. Gawaine tells the story of their grandmother, Igraine, the countess of Cornwall, whose husband was killed by Uther Pendragon so Pendragon could have Igraine as his wife. In the room below, Morgause is trying to turn herself invisible. She boils a live cat, separates the bones from the flesh, and then puts each bone into her mouth while watching herself in a mirror. Before she finds the right bone, however, she grows bored and throws the whole mess out the window. Above her, the boys promise that they will avenge the death of their grandfather by fighting Uther's son, Arthur.

SUMMARY: CHAPTER 2

Back in England, Arthur stands on the battlements of a castle with Merlyn. They discuss a recent battle with one of the Gaelic kings, King Lot of Orkney, who is Morgause's husband. Arthur is proud of his victories, but Merlyn scolds him for not knowing how many kerns, or foot soldiers, were killed in the battle. Merlyn also tells Arthur that he will have to start thinking for himself, because Merlyn knows that he will soon fall in love with a girl named Nimue, who will use Merlyn's own spells to trap him in a cave for several centuries. As Arthur holds a rock in his hands, he is awestruck by the fact that he could drop it on somebody's head down below and nobody could punish him. Merlyn watches Arthur intently while Arthur thinks about this power aloud, but Arthur breaks out of his bloodthirsty reverie and uses the stone to knock off Merlyn's hat.

SUMMARY: CHAPTER 3

One day, Kay, Merlyn, and Arthur go hunting for grouse. Merlyn explains that there are many reasons why the Gaelic kings are rebelling against Arthur. One of these is the long-running ethnic feud between the Gaels, an older race who once ruled England, and the Normans, who drove them out. Another is the fact that Arthur's father killed the count of Cornwall, who was the father of Queen Morgause, Morgan le Fay, and a woman named Elaine. Arthur says he understands why the Gaelic kings are fighting him. Merlyn retorts, however, that two wrongs do not make a right. Even though Merlyn is a Gael himself, he says the Gaels destroyed another race before they themselves were driven out, and that this conflict occurred so long ago that it is time to forget it.

SUMMARY: CHAPTER 4

Later, Merlyn argues that fighting is generally wrong, except in cases of self-defense. Kay is skeptical that the aggressor is always so easy to identify, but Merlyn stubbornly disagrees. He tells Arthur that his enemy, King Lot, the aggressor in this case, starts wars as casually as if he were fox hunting and has no regard for the common soldier.

SUMMARY: CHAPTER 5

In Orkney, Gawaine, Gareth, Gaheris, and Agravaine are visiting the house of Mother Morlan, a local woman. St. Toirdealbhach, a "relapsed saint," is also in the house. After a drink of whiskey, the fierce and battle-scarred old saint tells them the story of King Conor, who was shot in battle by a magic bullet. The ball lodged in his temple, and his surgeons told him to avoid all excitement. One day during a thunderstorm, a servant told King Conor that Jesus was being crucified that day, and as the king rushed to defend his savior, he fell down dead. St. Toirdealbhach thinks sadly that war isn't what it used to be and that battles have gotten so big that it is hard to remember what is being fought over. The boys protest that one needs many men in a battle or there would be no one to kill.

The boys ride a couple of donkeys to the beach, beating the donkeys furiously as they go. A magic barge lands, and three knights—King Pellinore, Sir Grummore, and Sir Palomides—descend with a dog. A crowd of local townspeople gathers around them.

ANALYSIS: CHAPTERS 1–5

In this section, White introduces the character of Morgause and, in doing so, shows the sharp contrast between the upbringing of the Orkney children and that of Arthur. We first meet Morgause when she is boiling a live cat to make herself invisible—not because she needs to become invisible, but because she is bored and wants to entertain herself. When the project is no longer amusing, Morgause gives it up, even though it seems as if she is only a few tries away from succeeding. Morgause is a markedly different parent than the kindly Sir Ector or Merlyn, and her children's values, even this early on, are likewise warped. St. Toirdealbhach, who is hardly a role model, yearns for the days when wars were more personal, but the Orkney boys are shocked at how smaller-scale warfare would reduce their chances of killing people. As they ride the donkeys, their goal is as much to hurt the beasts as it is to get to the beach. Disturbing as their comments and behavior are, we feel sorry for the boys. The first image of them—in which they whisper because they are never sure when they are doing something wrong—is so pathetic that we have to pity rather than dislike them.

We first find Gawaine, Gareth, Gaheris, and Agravaine telling each other the story about the murder of their grandfather and the seduction of their grandmother. Merlyn mentions this incident in his later discussions with Arthur, which demonstrates the importance of Pendragon's crime to the story and Arthur's destiny. In these first few chapters of the novel's second book, for example, the seduction of Igraine and the death of her husband are the only events that seem to connect Arthur with Orkney. If it weren't for these events, which neither Arthur nor the Orkneys actually witnessed, neither party would mention the other.

The relationship between Merlyn and Arthur has clearly changed, but Arthur continues to learn and develop throughout these chapters. Arthur is starting to be shaped by his role as a powerful king who wields power over others, and he initially wants to make war and seek glory. Merlyn makes Arthur see, however, that such goals are costly, most often for those who have the least say in them. He reminds Arthur of the lessons he learned during his childhood adventures. Accordingly, Arthur has a breakthrough when he understands for the first time that having a lot of power does not mean that you can determine morality or justice—that it is possible to have power and still be wrong. Merlyn acknowledges that war is not always wrong—that it is sometimes necessary—but Arthur slowly comes to the conclusion that aggression is always bad. From a contemporary perspective, some of this philosophy seems obvious. Some might also argue that White overstates the violence of medieval England, but it was certainly a society in which strength prevailed. The political philosophies of the Enlightenment were centuries away, and the land was largely lawless, much closer to the Wild West of nineteenth-century America than to the English monarchy as we envision it. Arthur's eventual grasp of the idea that power does not equal freedom from moral obligation is therefore quite revolutionary, an unusually gentle way of viewing the world.

Book II: "The Queen of Air and Darkness," Chapters 6–10

Summary: Chapter 6

> *Why can't you harness Might so that it works for Right? . . . The Might is there, in the bad half of people, and you can't neglect it.*
>
> (See QUOTATIONS, *p. 72*)

Arthur stops by Merlyn's room to ask his advice, but Merlyn tells him that the king should always summon people to him. Merlyn is summoned to the Royal Chamber an hour later, and he, Arthur,

Kay, and Sir Ector talk about the idea of chivalry. Arthur tells the others that might does not equal right and that currently, knights do whatever they please while the people slaughter, torture, and rape one another. For example, Arthur says, there are knights like Sir Bruce Sans Pitié, who rides around the country killing people and carrying off maidens for sport. Might can be used to achieve right, Arthur reasons, saying that he will use force to put down the Gaelic rebellion and then try to harness this power for good by creating an order of knights that will fight for just causes.

Summary: Chapter 7
Back in Orkney, King Pellinore, Sir Palomides, and Sir Grummore go hunting for a unicorn with Morgause, who is trying to make the three men fall in love with her. According to legend, a unicorn can be caught only if a virgin attracts it, but despite what the Orkney children think, Morgause does not fit the description. The boys visit St. Toirdealblach, who tells them another story about a witch. The Orkney boys decide to capture a unicorn to please their mother. They coerce a kitchen maid into playing the virgin, binding her to a tree in the forest. A unicorn appears and lays its head in the kitchen maid's lap with grace and majesty. Agravaine, seized by a fit of passion, kills the unicorn, yelling incoherently that the girl is his mother and the unicorn has dared to put its head in her lap. They take the unicorn's head home as a trophy, but Morgause fails to notice it, and when she learns what they have done, she has them whipped.

Summary: Chapter 8
On the plain of Bedegraine, before joining in battle with King Lot and his forces, Arthur, Merlyn, and Kay make further plans for Arthur's order of knights. Arthur decides that the knights should all sit at a round table, so that each of the places are equal. Merlyn informs Arthur that King Leodegrance, whose daughter, Guenever, eventually marries Arthur, has such a table. Merlyn also asks Arthur to remind him to warn Arthur about Guenever in the future. Kay tells Merlyn that he thinks it is right to start a war if he knows that a victory will bring a better life to the conquered people. Merlyn angrily tells Kay that it is much better to make ideas available than to force them on others. Trembling with rage, he tells Kay that he knows of an Austrian who shared Kay's views and dragged the whole world into bloody chaos.

SUMMARY: CHAPTER 9

Sir Palomides and Sir Grummore create a costume that looks like the Questing Beast and then convince King Pellinore that they have spotted the beast on the island. Meanwhile, Morgause, her advances spurned, decides that she hates the knights and that she loves her children. Gareth runs to bring the others the good news that they are forgiven, and he finds them squabbling. Agravaine wants to write their father a letter telling him that Morgause has been cheating on him with the English knights. This suggestion enrages Gawaine, and when Agravaine pulls a knife to defend himself, Gawaine almost kills him. That night, as Palomides and Grummore march in costume to lead Pellinore on a hunt, they run into the real Questing Beast. The beast mistakes them for another one of its species, falls in love, and chases them halfway up a cliff.

SUMMARY: CHAPTER 10

The night before the battle with King Lot, Merlyn reminds Arthur that he will marry Guenever and that he must be wary of the relationship between Guenever and Lancelot. He also tells Arthur a parable with the moral that no one can escape fate.

ANALYSIS: CHAPTERS 6–10

In this section, with the help of Kay, Sir Ector, and Merlyn, King Arthur continues to think about the ideology behind his reign, which he hopes will thrive on fairness. The Round Table is a symbol of this kind of government—a society so democratic that even the king's table is designed to prevent fighting and squabbling over status. This table is the culmination of all that Merlyn and his lessons have taught Arthur, even though Merlyn insists that Arthur will have to do some of the thinking for himself. Even though Arthur's idea is noble, however, the novel never treats the project as something glorious or easy. Rather, it appears to be a difficult and tricky idea to implement. Every time we see Arthur and his advisers discussing the idea of might versus right, they are trying to figure out a way around a new obstacle, and the chapters rarely end happily. Merlyn, who has so far been a compassionate and caring adviser to Arthur, does not seem interested in making things easy for the young king by allowing Arthur to compromise or adopt the system already in place. Instead, Merlyn is driven by the age-old feuds and ethnic hatreds that are tearing the country apart, and he almost seems to be using Arthur as a weapon to right old wrongs. Life for the people of England may soon improve, but we wonder if Arthur is dooming himself with his own ideas.

White includes a contemporary historical reference in the text. Kay argues that might can be used if a ruler discovers an improved way of life and the people are too stubborn to convert. Merlyn responds to Kay's theory with outrage, likening him to an unnamed Austrian who "tried to impose his reformation by the sword, and plunged the civilized world into misery and chaos." Since Merlyn lives backward in time, the fact that this incident occurred in his youth means that it occurred during our recent past. The incident is a clear reference to Adolf Hitler, who as the leader of Germany from 1933 to 1945, ordered the execution of million of Jews, as well as Gypsies, homosexuals, and others, during World War II. In a story that is several centuries old, White is again finding lessons and parables that are relevant to the modern era. The problems that Arthur is trying to solve, White warns, still exist, and he gives us contemporary examples to drive his message home.

The Orkney children are described again in this section; as their destructive behavior increases, so does our dislike for their mother, Morgause. White's biographer, Sylvia Townsend Warner, reports that White's publisher rejected the initial draft of this novel because Morgause was depicted far too negatively. Townsend Warner hypothesizes that while writing about Morgause, White was working through some of his feelings toward his own mother, whom he remembered as someone who was much more willing to take love than to give it. Although White subsequently rewrote most of the novel, toning down all the references to Morgause, some of the personal emotion that drove the first draft still shows up in several of the chapters. Agravaine's claim that the unicorn has somehow violated the children's mother supports Warner's psychological reading of the novel, since Agravaine's behavior shows an unhealthy fixation with his mother's sexual activity that far exceeds normal childish behavior. The other children also bear psychological scars, as can be seen in their earlier ill treatment of the donkeys, but they seem to be strong enough to withstand them better than Agravaine-does. Agravaine's character has already been so poisoned by his uncontrollable love for his mother that he is willing to pull a knife on his own brother. With the exception of Gareth, who is a sweet and sensitive child, the Orkney children fight in the most violent and disagreeable ways, but it is hard to feel anything but sorry for them since they have been so distorted by the evil Morgause.

The satire of knighthood, which begins in Book I with the portrayal of Pellinore's battle with Sir Grummore, continues here with the description of the silly and lighthearted adventures of Palomides, Pellinore, and Grummore. The adventures of the three knights also provide comic relief from the unhappiness that prevails in Morgause's castle. *The Once and Future King* is primarily a sad and contemplative novel, but it also tries to engage its readers, and the adventures of Palomides, Pellinore, and Grummore provide comic interludes that do not distract too much from the novel's weightier matters.

Book II: "The Queen of Air and Darkness," Chapters 11–14

Summary: Chapter 11
In Orkney, King Pellinore is walking along the beach when he comes across Sir Palomides and Sir Grummore trapped on a cliff ledge. They are still in costume, and the Questing Beast has fallen in love with what she thinks is her mate. She watches them adoringly from the foot of the cliff. Pellinore, unwilling to kill the beast, holds her by the tail while the two knights make a run for Morgause's castle. They make it safely into the castle, but the beast escapes from Pellinore and waits outside for them to exit. Pellinore returns to the castle with Piggy, the daughter of the queen of Flanders. She tells them that she and the Questing Beast rode the magic barge from Flanders to find Pellinore. Their joy at being reunited is not shared by the inhabitants of the castle, since it appears that the Questing Beast intends to wait outside until what she thinks is her mate comes outside.

Summary: Chapter 12
In his great battle against Lot and the rest of the Gaels at Bedegraine, Arthur ignores the knightly rules of war: he attacks during the night and attacks the knights directly, ignoring the foot soldiers. Arthur's army is much smaller than the Gaelic kings', but his forces swell when he calls in his allies, two French kings named Bors and Ban. The French kings bring their armies to support Arthur in exchange for help with their own battles in France. With the help, Arthur's army swiftly defeats the Gaelic army.

Summary: Chapter 13
Back in Orkney, the Questing Beast continues to guard outside the castle. King Lot's defeated army returns home, and Sir Pellinore, Sir

Ector, and Sir Grummore are surprised to learn that England and Orkney have been at war. Merlyn stops by, looking sleek and happy because he has begun a fateful love affair with Nimue. The knights ask Merlyn for advice on how to make the Questing Beast go away, but Merlyn is troubled because he cannot remember a particular warning he wants to give Arthur and can only tell them to psychoanalyze the beast. Under the pretense of reconciliation, Morgause makes plans to travel to England with her children. As she packs, she sinisterly fingers her spancel, a magic tape made of human flesh that is designed to make men fall in love with her.

SUMMARY: CHAPTER 14

> It is why Sir Thomas Malory called his very long book the Death of Arthur. . . . It is the tragedy . . . of sin coming home to roost.
>
> (See QUOTATIONS, p. 73)

Morgause, her children, and the English knights make the journey to England. King Arthur, who still has fond childhood memories of Pellinore, has prepared an extravagant marriage for Pellinore and Piggy. Meanwhile, in North Humberland, Merlyn suddenly remembers what he has forgotten to tell Arthur: his mother was Igraine, who was also the mother of Morgan le Fay and Morgause. Thus, Morgause is Arthur's half-sister, and Gawaine, Agravaine, Gaheris, and Gareth are his nephews. Merlyn is too sleepy and muddled to take care of the problem immediately, however, and before Merlyn can warn Arthur, Morgause uses the spancel and her own charms to get Arthur to sleep with her. Nine months later, she gives birth to their son, Mordred. The narrator notes that what makes the Arthurian story so tragic is that a simple, unwitting mistake by Arthur tears him and his dreams apart many years later.

ANALYSIS: CHAPTERS 11–14

King Arthur's battle with King Lot is strange since it seems to lack a real sense of glory or triumph and appears more methodical instead. There is no honor in the way that Arthur wins his victory, primarily because he attacks at night, when few of his enemies are fully armored. As treacherous as this attack might strike us, however, we still want Arthur to win, and his sneakiness seems far preferable to the cruelty of earlier wars. Arthur has a clear purpose in battling King Lot's knights; he is not just indulging in the thoughtless slaughter of foot soldiers. Because he has a mission, we can understand his desire to sidestep the code that has made war into a sporting event for so many years. If Arthur hurt the weak foot soldiers, he would be acting cruelly. Therefore, the fact that the description of the battle feels more bureaucratic than military can be read as a sign that Arthur's vision of glorious peace is well under way.

In an interesting footnote, the number of kings participating in the battle vividly illustrates why England has been so torn apart by civil war. Most of the knights on each side are barons, but a number of Arthur's enemies are also kings. Lot, for example, is king of Orkney. So many of Arthur's enemies call themselves kings that the term appears to have lost all meaning for them—one of them, the king of the Hundred Knights, does not even seem to have a territory to call his own. Our contemporary understanding of the word king is of a monarch who controls a vast expanse of land and is the only person in the empire who has such a title. In the world Arthur has inherited, however, king is a common title, which indicates how many of Arthur's rivals consider themselves so powerful that they answer to no one else.

Family ties are generally viewed as an integral source of support for a struggling monarch, but Arthur's seduction by Morgause reveals that family can be a source of destruction. Until now, Morgause's connection to Arthur has been murky. There are hints, earlier in the novel, that they are related, but White hopes that Morgause's relation to Arthur will be as much of a mystery to us as it is to Arthur. We have seen Morgause only as the cruel mother of four unruly boys and the seductive hostess of several silly English knights. Suddenly, however, she is revealed to be Arthur's half-sister. This news does not bring about a reconciliation between them but rather transforms Morgause into a figure of destruction. Although Arthur's reign has barely begun and is yet to see its most glorious years, his affair with Morgause is the first step in the reign's collapse. The incest is not intentional, at least not on Arthur's part, but it is a sin so grave that ultimately he cannot escape punishment for it. Arthur's project to build a just and lawful kingdom is doomed before it even begins. This tragedy is heightened by the fact that his downfall is brought about by his own friends and family. The instruments of Arthur's destruction are Morgause, his half-sister; Agravaine and Mordred, his nephews; Guenever, his wife; and Lancelot, his best friend.

BOOK III: "THE ILL-MADE KNIGHT," CHAPTERS 1–6

SUMMARY: CHAPTER 1

King Ban's son Lancelot is skilled at games, but horribly ugly. Arthur once explained to the young Lancelot his attempt to end the principle of might makes right and asked Lancelot if he wanted to help Arthur do so when he was older. Lancelot said he would indeed like to join Arthur. Fiercely dedicated to Arthur, Lancelot committed himself to a life of training.

SUMMARY: CHAPTER 2

Uncle Dap, an expert on all things related to knighthood, trains Lancelot. For three years Lancelot does nothing but learn about knighthood and practice sword fighting and jousting. The narrator says that Lancelot will eventually go on to be the greatest knight in Arthur's court. Lancelot practices by finding the weak points on armor, lifting weights, and sparring against his brother and cousins in mock swordfights with strict rules.

SUMMARY: CHAPTER 3

One day, Merlyn tells Lancelot that Lancelot will be the best knight in the world. He explains that Arthur has married a woman named Guenever and that Arthur already has one hundred knights at his Round Table. Lancelot is disappointed that Arthur has not invited him to join the table. Merlyn appears with his beloved Nimue, and they vanish for a sort of magical honeymoon. Lancelot decides to leave for England immediately.

SUMMARY: CHAPTER 4

Uncle Dap accompanies Lancelot as his squire. On their way to Arthur's castle, in Camelot, they encounter a knight in black armor who challenges Lancelot to a joust. Lancelot defeats the knight, who turns out to be King Arthur. Arthur is thrilled to see Lancelot and knights him back at Camelot. At first, Lancelot is jealous of Guenever because he is fiercely protective of his friendship with Arthur and thinks she is coming between them. Guenever tries to be friendly despite Lancelot's rejection, but one day he lashes out at her. Once Lancelot sees that he has hurt Guenever's feelings, he no longer sees her as an evil interloper.

SUMMARY: CHAPTER 5

Lancelot and Guenever, reconciled, now spend more time together. Uncle Dap and Lancelot argue about Lancelot and Guenever's relationship, and Lancelot ultimately says that Uncle Dap can remain in Camelot only if he refrains from insinuating anything about Lancelot and Guenever. Arthur is too kind to believe rumors of this relationship, having managed to bury Merlyn's warning in the back of his mind. To erase his doubt, Arthur decides to bring Lancelot with him to fight the Romans. Lancelot is angry that he is not left behind to guard Guenever, but he goes nonetheless. The war lasts several years—Arthur eventually becomes the overlord of most of Europe, with Lancelot as his new champion and friend.

SUMMARY: CHAPTER 6

> [H]e had a contradictory nature which was far from
> holy. . . . For one thing, he liked to hurt people.
> *(See* QUOTATIONS, *p. 74)*

Lancelot and Arthur return to England determined that nothing can divide them, and they are welcomed with great cheer. When Guenever greets them, however, it becomes clear to Lancelot that she can indeed come between him and Arthur. If he were a less principled man, the narrator says, Lancelot might simply run off with Guenever. Instead, he fights his attraction. But since he cannot stand to be around Guenever when Arthur is around, he decides to leave the court and go on a quest.

ANALYSIS: CHAPTERS 1–6

In the third book of *The Once and Future King*, White introduces Lancelot, a staple figure of English literature; however, White takes a very different approach to the great knight than that of the romantic interpretations we are used to seeing. Traditionally, Lancelot is a handsome and brave fighter, and his affair with Guenever, while forbidden, is portrayed as sweepingly romantic and passionate. White offers no such portrayal. From the very beginning, everything about the Lancelot he shows us is painful and distorted. As a young boy, Lancelot is incredibly ugly, and although he is touchingly loyal to Arthur, he is a sullen loner. Even the title of the book, "The Ill-Made Knight," signifies a character who is poorly put together. Lancelot is a talented fighter, but this quality never seems to be particularly great or triumphant. Instead, it appears as though Lancelot fights well because he is incapable of anything else. Furthermore, everything that Lancelot does to escape his fate only traps him further in it. By immersing himself in quests to try to forget Guenever, Lancelot becomes a hero, which in turn makes her fall more in love with him.

The similarities between Lancelot and King Arthur highlight the eventual contrast in how each man reacts to Guenever's infidelity. Each grows up an outsider: Arthur is a runtish orphan dubbed "the Wart," while Lancelot suffers insults for his ugliness. Frustrations of youth spur both men to hone their natural talents: Arthur engages in political discussions with Merlyn; Lancelot pursues chivalric ideals under the tutelage of Uncle Dap. Arthur and Lancelot are both outsiders pursuing abstract systems of individual perfection—one political wisdom, the other chivalry—and, respecting each other's commitment to personal excellence, they develop a close friendship. Lancelot's eventual treachery with Guenever is insidious because it is a betrayal of a friendship and of the values on which that friendship is established. Arthur's esteem for others and his trust in their adherence to a shared code proves to be his undoing, because he cannot suspect his wife and good friend of transgressing this code.

Book III: "The Ill-Made Knight," Chapters 7–9

Summary: Chapter 7

On one quest, Lancelot rescues Gawaine, who has been captured by an evil knight named Sir Carados. Later, left alone one morning at the home of his cousin, Sir Lionel, Lancelot is captured by four queens—one of whom is Morgan le Fay—but he refuses their demands to take one of them as his mistress. He escapes with the help of the girl who serves his meals, and in exchange, he agrees to fight in a tournament on behalf of her father, King Bagdemagus.

Fighting with a shield that has no insignia so no one will recognize him, Lancelot steers King Bagdemagus's side to victory in the tournament. Lancelot then sets out to find Lionel. He discovers that Sir Turquine, Sir Carados's brother, has captured Lionel and sixty-three other knights. Lancelot and Turquine fight a fierce battle, and Turquine is so impressed by Lancelot, whom he does not recognize, that he agrees to release his captives as long as the unfamiliar knight is not Lancelot. Lancelot informs Turquine of his identity, and after fighting for two more hours, manages to kill him. Gaheris is among the freed captives, and he marvels at how Lancelot keeps helping the Orkneys. Another of the captives, he tells Lancelot, is Agravaine.

SUMMARY: CHAPTER 8

One day in the summer, a beautiful lady asks Lancelot to climb a tree to retrieve her falcon. When Lancelot removes his armor, the lady's husband, a fat knight, attacks him. The fat knight is a member of the upper classes losing power under Arthur's rule, and he refuses to listen to Lancelot's pleas for a fair fight. Lancelot eventually kills the fat knight. Later, Lancelot meets a knight who is trying to kill his own wife for adultery. Lancelot rides between them, but the knight tricks Lancelot into looking in a different direction and then cuts off the wife's head. The knight then begs for mercy, and Lancelot, unable to kill a man begging for his life, spares him. Lancelot has a number of other adventures, and he always sends his prisoners back to Arthur's court, at Carlion, to bow before Guenever rather than before Arthur.

SUMMARY: CHAPTER 9

Guenever is pleased at these signs of Lancelot's love, and she is so swept away by them that when Lancelot returns, they are drawn to each other instantly. She still loves Arthur, but with a sort of awed affection. While Lancelot tries to repress his feelings, Arthur worries that his knights have become too fixated with what he calls "games-mania," in which every knight compares his prowess to everyone else's. He worries particularly about the Orkneys, whose father, Lot, was accidentally killed by Pellinore. Now that her husband is dead, Morgause is trying to seduce every knight she can, and the Orkney knights are becoming uncontrollable as a result.

ANALYSIS: CHAPTERS 7–9

With Lancelot's adventures, White gets to the heart of the Arthurian tradition, but his interpretation of the classic stories goes in a purposefully different direction. Malory's influence on White is more apparent here than in any of the novel's other books, and he is cited in almost every one of Lancelot's quests. Even Malory's fifteenth-century language colors White's narrative. On Lancelot's first adventure, when he finds Gawaine held captive by Sir Carados, Gawaine tells Lancelot that his current situation is "Never so hard, unless that ye help me, for without ye rescue me, I know nae knight that may." In earlier passages, Gawaine speaks modern English with a Scottish accent, but this snippet of dialogue written in archaic English is taken straight out of Malory's fifteenth-century text. All of the later episodes in Chapters 7 and 8 are told, with matching details, in Malory's *Morte d'Arthur*. In the first two books of the novel, White tries to produce his own version of the Arthurian legend. But the first chapters of "The Ill-Made Knight," the third book, try more specifically to interpret Malory's work on King Arthur. These chapters take events from Malory's Arthurian story and, without changing any details, make us wonder if there is more to them than Malory might have thought.

This third book elaborates on the evil knight, a topic that is only hinted at earlier in the novel. Arthur has enemies in earlier chapters, most notably King Lot, but these early enemies are primarily motivated by power rather than a difference in ideology. Early on, we hear about the old philosophy of might makes right, but we do not see examples of this idea until now. Sir Carados and Sir Turquine are both prime examples. They ride around the country and take knights hostage for their own amusement. They are variations on the character of Sir Bruce Sans Pitié, the backstabbing knight who is mentioned, but never appears in earlier chapters. Even kings such as Lot follow certain rules, but now we see knighthood at its most corrupt, used only to bully other people. Chapter 8 presents two more examples, even more appalling, of this abuse. One knight uses his lady to persuade Lancelot to scale a tree, and then he tries to kill Lancelot with no armor or weapons handy. The other knight takes advantage of Lancelot's gullibility to cut off his own wife's head. A number of Arthur's knights, including Gawaine, Agravaine, and Kay, seem petty and malicious, and we may wonder what they are doing at Arthur's court. In comparison to the figures in Chapter 8, however, Gawaine and his companions shine, and we can see why Arthur might enlist them to put down worse tyrants.

BOOK III: "THE ILL-MADE KNIGHT," CHAPTERS 10–15

SUMMARY: CHAPTER 10

Lancelot is unable to act on his love for Guenever because his religion and Arthur's own principles about fairness and justice, in which Lancelot believes deeply, forbid him to do so. While everyone else thinks Lancelot is a great man, he hates himself.

SUMMARY: CHAPTER 11

Lancelot stays at Arthur's court in Camelot for several weeks, but he cannot bring himself to do anything about Guenever. He is afraid that if he sleeps with her, he will lose his strength and his position as Arthur's best knight. Uncle Dap advises him to go on another quest, so he makes his way to the haunted castle of Corbin, which is owned by King Pelles. On the way, Lancelot is stopped by villagers who tell him that fairies, among them Morgan le Fay, have put a spell on a local girl and placed her in a vat of boiling water, from which she can be saved only by the best knight in the world. Lancelot tries to refuse, but they insist, and he ends up pulling a naked young woman named Elaine out of the vat. Afterward, they are greeted by Elaine's father, who turns out to be King Pelles. Pelles invites Lancelot to stay. Excited by Elaine's great beauty, Lancelot cannot yet understand that he has performed a miracle.

SUMMARY: CHAPTER 12

At the castle of Corbin, Lancelot is miserable and thinks of Guenever. Pelles's butler cheers Lancelot with wine. While Lancelot is intoxicated, Pelles's butler tells Lancelot that Guenever is staying at a nearby castle, waiting for Lancelot. Lancelot rushes off to see her. The next morning, he wakes up and sees that the woman in bed with him is Elaine. Realizing that he has been tricked, Lancelot threatens to kills Elaine. He thinks that his strength lies in his virginity and that he will now no longer be able to work miracles or be the best knight. Elaine tells Lancelot that she loves him and wishes to bear his child, whom she will name Galahad. Lancelot says that since she tricked him the baby will be hers alone and that he is leaving.

SUMMARY: CHAPTER 13

At Camelot, Guenever thinks of Lancelot as she stitches a new shield cover for Arthur. Convinced that Elaine has ruined him, Lancelot sees no point in not furthering his destruction, and he races up the stairs to Guenever. Before they realize what is happening, they have slept together.

SUMMARY: CHAPTER 14

King Ban, Lancelot's father, is under attack and writes Arthur to ask for help. Arthur leaves for France after asking Lancelot to stay behind and guard his kingdom. While Arthur is away, Lancelot and Guenever spend twelve happy months together. Lancelot tells Guenever that when he was little, he was a very holy little boy, always punishing himself for the slightest faults. Lancelot tells Guenever that he originally stayed away from her because he was worried that by sleeping with her he would lose his ability to perform miracles. He adds that he is giving her his God-given gifts as a present for her love, and that he does not regret it.

SUMMARY: CHAPTER 15

When Guenever learns, however, that Elaine has given birth to a baby boy named Galahad—Lancelot's first name—she realizes that Lancelot and Elaine have slept together. Hurt, Guenever becomes petulant, lashing out at Lancelot and threatening to have Elaine executed. Eventually, Lancelot and Guenever are tearfully reconciled, but a seed of hatred and distrust has been planted in their love affair.

ANALYSIS: CHAPTERS 10–15

Lancelot is conflicted by two contradictory passions—his love for Guenever and his love for Arthur and chivalry. Elaine's sudden appearance makes balancing these two passions impossible. Already, everything that Lancelot does to try to distance himself from Guenever only deepens his love for her, but at least he has managed to keep his two worlds separate. He is always an unsatisfied lover, but on his earlier quests, he is also a knight and can take refuge in a world that is all about fighting and ethics. Once he meets Elaine, however, even this line becomes blurred. His quests can no longer honestly be said to be about fighting and remedying injustice, since his tryst with Elaine has filled them with the kind of amorous intrigue from which he has been running. The effects of this tryst are irreversible. Among other things, Lancelot loses, or at least thinks he has lost, his power to perform miracles, since only virgins are supposed to be allowed to perform miracles. Even on a less mystical level, sleeping with Elaine has so contaminated Lancelot's quest that he thinks of his entire knighthood as having been corrupted and ruined. Now that Lancelot's two worlds have been forced to mingle, Lancelot sees no reason not to ruin them altogether, and rushes into Guenever's arms.

The figure of Elaine in these chapters, as well as our developing understanding of Guenever's character, raises some questions about the novel's treatment of women. As much as *The Once and Future King* seems to be a rejection of the machismo of earlier Arthurian tales, it is very much a man's world, where even the best-intentioned women have a destructive effect. Guenever and Elaine are certainly not as evil or unlikable as Morgause, whom the novel portrays quite misogynistically. Nonetheless, the novel treats Guenever and Elaine more like the Orkney family than like Arthur or Lancelot. Like Gawaine, Guenever and Elaine have good hearts, but their circumstances force them to be petty, demanding, and conniving, whereas Lancelot and Arthur are still portrayed as selfless and noble. The novel explains that Guenever has good reason for her behavior, but she is still overwhelmingly depicted as mean and spiteful. Elaine is described as a sweet girl who is smitten by Lancelot, but she tricks him and her demands on him only increase with time. To a certain extent, these are flattering portrayals of both women, allowing them to be human beings instead of boring, saintly figures. Since the story of Arthur was written well before White wrote *The Once and Future King*, he had only a limited amount of room to shape his plot without veering away from the Arthurian canon. One could argue, however, that the novel still treats women disrespectfully and that, however objective White may want to be, we cannot help but despise his two main female characters.

BOOK III: "THE ILL-MADE KNIGHT," CHAPTERS 16–20

SUMMARY: CHAPTER 16

> [Arthur] was hoping to weather the trouble by refusing to become conscious of it.
>
> *(See* QUOTATIONS, *p. 75)*

Arthur, back from France, realizes that something is wrong at Camelot. One day, he brings up the subject of Guenever with Lancelot, but it is an awkward moment, and the affair is not directly addressed. Lancelot then bumps into Guenever, who tells him Elaine is on her way. Guenever seems to be on the verge of reconciling herself with Lancelot, but she then tears herself away from him, saying that she does not want to stand in his way if he discovers that he wishes to marry Elaine.

SUMMARY: CHAPTER 17

Guenever cordially welcomes Elaine, who brings Galahad, though some hostility is evident. Lancelot avoids Elaine and Galahad until Guenever orders him to go to them. Guenever adds, however, that

Lancelot is not to sleep with Elaine. Lancelot says he has no intention of doing so. He is fascinated by the sight of his son, but when Elaine tries to embrace Lancelot, Lancelot rushes out of the room.

SUMMARY: CHAPTER 18

The next day, Lancelot and Elaine are summoned to Guenever's chamber. Lancelot goes happily, remembering how he was summoned the night before to Guenever's room, where they spent the night together. Guenever, however, is furious, and she accuses Lancelot of sleeping with Elaine. Elaine defends Lancelot, saying that she thought he was sleeping with Guenever, and Lancelot realizes that he has been tricked once again. Guenever refuses to believe Elaine's story. Lancelot suddenly jumps out the window and flees the castle. Elaine bitterly accuses Guenever of having driven Lancelot mad.

SUMMARY: CHAPTER 19

Two years later, King Pelles's friend Sir Bliant tells him of a wild man he once encountered, who he thinks may have been Lancelot. The wild man was naked, but spoke in the high tongue and was so good with a sword that he managed to knock out Sir Bliant, who was in armor. The wild man then ran to Sir Bliant's tent, jumped into his bed, and fell asleep. While the wild man was sleeping, Sir Bliant brought him to his castle. A year and a half after that first encounter, Sir Bliant was attacked by two evil knights, one of whom was Sir Bruce Sans Pitié. The wild man saw this attack from his window, broke his handcuffs, and saved Sir Bliant. Sir Bliant and Pelles speculate that it may have been Lancelot.

SUMMARY: CHAPTER 20

Soon after, a wild man comes to Pelles's castle. Pelles asks the wild man if he is Lancelot, but all the man does is roar. Pelles tells his servants to give the wild man the clothes of a fool and keep him locked in the stable. One night, Pelles gets drunk and gives the wild man his cloak. In this royal clothing, the wild man looks brave and noble, and the servants make a path for him as he walks out.

ANALYSIS: CHAPTERS 16–20

This sudden mingling of Lancelot's worlds—his relationship with Elaine and his relationship with Guenever—turns out to have disastrous results for Lancelot's psyche. Now that questing and chivalry have been contaminated for him, Lancelot has nowhere to hide from Guenever, with the result being that he goes insane. Lancelot, who is admittedly a little slow to learn, is tricked for a second time and finds that what he thought of as a reconciliation in fact serves to drive him and his love apart. He cannot, however, simply rush out on a series of quests, as he does earlier; his first encounter with Elaine has taught him that even adventures and questing can be soured by love. When Guenever turns on Lancelot, therefore, he is defenseless, unable to derive pleasure from the questing that earlier brings him comfort, or at least distraction. Without any way of escaping the pain he feels from Guenever's rage, Lancelot becomes insane from the strain.

Arthur's goodness in these chapters comes under close scrutiny, and we begin to wonder if his ignorance can sometimes be harmful. This is the case in Chapter 16, when Arthur fails to talk to Lancelot about Lancelot's affair with Guenever, avoiding the sort of honest confrontation that the issue so desperately needs. Arthur knows about the affair, but he is so dogmatic about the power of justice and goodwill that he remains purposefully blind to the issues that eventually tear his kingdom apart. But by abiding so rigidly to his principles, Arthur also violates his own laws. Just as Guenever and Lancelot are breaking the rules of honor, Arthur also cannot bear to follow the demands of his own laws, which would require that he punish them for their transgressions. By trying to be noble and selfless, Arthur and Lancelot enter, in a sense, a pact of dishonesty, by which they try to preserve Camelot with lies rather than with friendship.

Book III: "The Ill-Made Knight," Chapters 21–29

Summary: Chapter 21

Elaine has decided to become a nun and does not think much about Lancelot anymore. One day, she comes across the wild man asleep in her father's robe and immediately recognizes him as Lancelot. She tells King Pelles, and he summons doctors to heal Lancelot's spirits. Lancelot finally wakes from his madness, completely unconscious of anything that has occurred since he went berserk.

Summary: Chapter 22

Lancelot and Elaine eventually move into Sir Bliant's castle, and Lancelot goes by the name of Le Chevalier Mal Fet, which means "the ill-made knight." A young knight tells Lancelot that he has uncovered Lancelot's true identity. Lancelot asks him to respect his wish to remain incognito. The young knight apologetically promises to keep Lancelot's secret.

SUMMARY: CHAPTER 23

In the spring, Elaine arranges a huge tournament. Lancelot, in disguise, defeats everyone else at the tournament, and the others leave, grumbling about the mystery knight. Elaine cries at this social fiasco, then finds Lancelot standing on the castle ramparts, where she sees that the symbol on his shield is that of a knight bowing before a queen. One day, two knights come to Bliant Castle and ask to fight with the mysterious Chevalier Mal Fet. They are amazed by his prowess, and he eventually reveals that he is Lancelot. The two knights turn out to be Sir Degalis, one of the Round Table knights, and Sir Ector de Maris, who, not to be confused with Arthur's old guardian, is one of Arthur's knights and also Lancelot's brother. Elaine watches the joyful reunion, knowing that these knights will break her heart by taking Lancelot away.

SUMMARY: CHAPTER 24

Sir Degalis and Sir Ector de Maris urge Lancelot to return to Camelot with them. Lancelot feels doggedly obliged to Elaine and says he will return. One day, a squire appears and sits at the castle moat, saying he is waiting for Lancelot. Elaine asks Lancelot what she should do about Galahad if Lancelot does not return. Pretending not to know what she is talking about, Lancelot assures her he will return. The squire turns out be Uncle Dap, who has brought all of Lancelot's armor, polished and patched. Guenever has stitched a mantle onto the back of his helmet, and when he sniffs it, Lancelot is reminded of her. He rides away with Uncle Dap without looking back.

SUMMARY: CHAPTER 25

Fifteen years pass and England has grown much more civilized. Instead of thieves and murderers and towers going up in flames, the new civilization has scholars and hospitals. Arthur is now accepted as a great king, and Lancelot as a legendary hero. A new and eager generation of knights comes to Camelot, among them Gareth and Arthur's son, Mordred.

SUMMARY: CHAPTER 26

Arthur tells Lancelot a little about the Orkney boys and describes how they are so violent and unhappy because of Morgause. Of Morgause's children, Lancelot thinks the least of Mordred, though he is unaware that Morded is Arthur's son. Lancelot casually tells

Arthur that Morgause has seduced King Pellinore's youngest son, Lamorak. Arthur is aghast—it turns out that Pellinore killed Lot by accident in a tournament and was in turn killed by one of the Orkney clan. Arthur worries that Lamorak may be in danger.

Gareth enters crying and tells Arthur and Lancelot that Agravaine has killed their mother after finding her in bed with Lamorak. He adds that Agravaine, Mordred, and Gawaine have hunted down Lamorak as well.

SUMMARY: CHAPTER 27

Gawaine and Mordred return to Camelot. Gawaine still thinks Lamorak got what he deserved, but he feels bad about violating Arthur's principles. Mordred is more evil, and he asks the king for pardon only with great insolence. Arthur halfheartedly forgives them and orders them to leave. To strengthen the weakening Round Table, Arthur decides to send his knights on a quest for the Holy Grail, the copper cup or platter, according to medieval legend, from which Christ ate at the Last Supper. Lancelot then learns that Galahad is about to be knighted.

SUMMARY: CHAPTER 28

After two years, the knights who give up the search for the Holy Grail straggle back to Camelot. Gawaine is the first to return, and he does so in a bad mood, having come across no traces of the Holy Grail. He speaks bitterly of Galahad, who seems to be a knight of great piety, which Gawaine mistakes for arrogance. Gawaine shakes his head at the fact that Galahad does not eat meat or drink alcohol and is a virgin. Gawaine recounts how he and his companions slew seven knights laying siege to a castle of maidens, only to find that Galahad had already beaten them without having to kill anyone. In two hermitages, Gawaine reports, the priests lectured him for killing too many people and failing to repent. Arthur listens patiently, observing that Gawaine does seem to have been more interested in bloody adventures than in finding the Holy Grail.

SUMMARY: CHAPTER 29

Sir Lionel returns next and talks with a mixture of love and exasperation about the adventures of his brother, Sir Bors. According to Lionel, Bors's honor was tested by a series of trials. In the first of these, Bors defeated a knight without taking his life. Bors was then forced to choose between rescuing a maiden or saving Lionel himself, and he chose the strange woman over his brother. Then a fiend in disguise told Bors that unless he slept with a certain lady, she would kill herself; Bors refused, however, even when she threatened to kill her servants as well. Guenever is particularly appalled by this part of the story. A while later, Bors and Lionel met again, and Lionel, enraged that his brother chose to rescue the maiden instead of him, tried to kill Bors. Bors refused to fight back, even after Lionel killed a hermit and another knight who was trying to help Bors. As Lionel was on the verge of killing Bors, God came between them, and they made up. Lionel expresses regret for his killings and remarks that if anyone is pure enough to find the Holy Grail, it is Bors.

―――――――――

ANALYSIS: CHAPTERS 21–29

Until now, the third book has centered exclusively on Lancelot, but once he returns to sanity, the narrative switches tracks to tell us how much the rest of the kingdom has changed during Lancelot's absence. The tone of these chapters is a strange combination of optimism and apprehension. The violence and brutality of the past are quite vividly recollected, and White paints disturbing pictures of murders and wars, drawing on classic writers of the period such as Geoffrey Chaucer, the fourteenth-century English poet who wrote *The Canterbury Tales*. The book's present is described in far more gratifying terms, but there is a sense that this tranquility is temporary. We hear of newly safe roads and of scholars sitting down to write learned texts, but shortly after the novel describes these improvements, Arthur is mourning the fact that his kingdom will soon crumble. This peaceful period is fleeting; though we have just gotten to know England as a tranquil place, we are already being told that this peace will soon be gone.

Arthur's vision of a peaceful kingdom is a noble one, but his idea of harnessing might for right has limits that reveal themselves during the quest for the Holy Grail. Now that England has been civilized, Arthur's knights are still chomping at the bit for action. Arthur needs to keep coming up with ways to keep them occupied, but this plan cannot go on forever. The quest for the Holy Grail, as told by Gawaine and Lionel, proves that harnessing might on behalf of right is not enough, and that true tranquility lies in dispensing with force altogether. Gawaine and Lionel are integral members of the Round Table—both of them are faithful to Arthur's ideas—but they are not worthy of the Holy Grail because they still rely on violence as a way of life. Galahad emerges as the most perfect knight, in part because of his chaste and austere ways, but even more so because he is more interested in sparing lives than in taking them. The same can be said for Lionel's brother, Sir Bors. What both Gawaine and Lionel have never understood is that even killing justly is worse than not killing at all. The fundamental flaw in Arthur's plan is that it tries to steer violent men to use their talents for the common good, when true good, the kind that is needed to find the Holy Grail, can be achieved only by abandoning violence altogether.

Overall, *The Once and Future King* is more sympathetic to what Arthur is trying to achieve than to the perfection represented by the Holy Grail. Both Galahad and Bors are very holy and noble, but they also seem selfish. Bors refuses to fight his Lionel, even though other people die as a result of Lionel's sins. Gawaine tells us that Galahad defeats his own father, Lancelot, and is generally cold to the other knights. White's vision of the otherworldly perfection of the Holy Grail feels very clinical: the Holy Grail's champions may be perfect, but we feel very removed from them.

Book III: "The Ill-Made Knight," Chapters 30–37

Summary: Chapter 30

Sir Aglovale returns to Camelot and swears revenge on the Orkney faction for having killed his brother Lamorak. Arthur convinces Aglovale that the only way to stop the bloodshed is for him to give up on revenge. Aglovale tells Arthur about the adventures of his youngest brother, Sir Percival, who is also a holy knight like Galahad. Percival has some adventures in a magical forest and then boards a magical barge with Sir Bors and Sir Galahad. In the barge, they are joined by Percival's sister, a holy nun. On their search for the Holy Grail, the three knights get into a fight with a group of men and slaughter them. Galahad tells them the slaughter is not sinful, since the murdered men were not christened. They then come to another castle, where Percival's sister sacrifices her life to save a woman with a fatal disease. After telling his stories, Aglovale asks Arthur to invite the Orkneys to dinner on his behalf.

Summary: Chapter 31

Other returning knights bring contradicting rumors about the adventures of Bors, Percival, and Galahad. Rumors fly that Lancelot has died or gone mad. Guenever becomes less cautious, and Mordred and Agravaine wait eagerly for her to reveal her affair.

Lancelot returns to Camelot exhausted but sane. Uncle Dap tells Arthur that Lancelot has been wearing a hair shirt—a painful way of doing penance for one's sins.

SUMMARY: CHAPTER 32

The next day, Lancelot tells Arthur and Guenever the story of his search for the Holy Grail. Guenever, now forty-two years old, has dressed up and put on makeup in an effort to look good for Lancelot, and his heart warms at the sight of her. Lancelot tells them that he did not find the Holy Grail, which was reserved for Galahad. Lancelot also says that if Galahad seems cold, it is because he is more angelic than human. Lancelot relates that Galahad defeated him in jousting. Lancelot then confessed his sins, which he thought would make him the best knight in the world again. But he was then beaten by another group of knights, after which he fell asleep in a chapel. When he woke up, his sword and armor had been taken from him. He then began to wear the hair shirt as penance. Thinking he had cleansed himself and could fight as well as he had before, Lancelot fought a knight dressed in black but was again defeated.

SUMMARY: CHAPTER 33

Arthur is outraged that Lancelot, his best knight, has been beaten. Lancelot continues with his story: he then got on a magic barge, and Galahad soon joined him. Eventually Galahad got out to seek the Holy Grail. The barge eventually returned to the castle where the Grail was located, and Lancelot was allowed to watch Galahad and other holy knights participate in a Mass in a chapel that contains the Holy Grail.

SUMMARY: CHAPTER 34

Having found God, Lancelot decides to end his affair with Guenever, but she is confident he will return to her. The narrator explains that Guenever is not an evil seductress, for seductresses usually leave men hollow, while both the men that Guenever loves have accomplished great things.

SUMMARY: CHAPTER 35

Guenever's faith in Lancelot's love grows weaker as time passes. One day, she demands that he go on another quest instead of torturing her with his presence. Just as Lancelot has decided to give up his abstinence and rekindle his affair with Guenever, she leaves the room and refuses to talk to him. He leaves Camelot the next morning.

SUMMARY: CHAPTER 36

With Lancelot gone, it becomes even clearer that Camelot is no longer the place it once was. The best knights have either succeeded in finding the Holy Grail or have died. At the court, fashions are silly and infidelity is the norm. Mordred and his friends now dominate Camelot, and Guenever is widely despised. In an attempt to win some popularity, she throws a dinner party for the knights and leaves out a tray of apples, Gawaine's favorite fruit. A distant relative of the Pellinores tries to avenge Lamorak's death by poisoning one of the apples, but an innocent knight eats one first and dies. Guenever is accused of trying to poison Gawaine. Each side picks a champion to fight for their cause.

SUMMARY: CHAPTER 37

Sir Bors agrees, reluctantly, to be Guenever's champion. In the days before the fight, however, he finds Lancelot in a nearby abbey. Lancelot takes Bors's place and easily defeats the knight who accused Guenever. He spares the knight's life, but insists that no mention of the incident be made on the poisoned knight's tombstone.

ANALYSIS: CHAPTERS 30–37

The episode with Sir Aglovale in Chapter 30 is important because it reveals that, even after it has been in place for so long, King Arthur's government still relies on sacrifices made for the common good. Arthur has committed himself to a system of government that is moral, but he has also inherited a country in which wrongs are committed every day and the system of justice in place is still not strong enough to deal with all of them. Arthur is not yet in a position to punish his strong men, so he must appeal to individuals such as Aglovale to forego their vengeance. The old system is based on avenging any wrongs that a person commits against one's family. The system is so ingrained that Arthur has to ask some of his knights to forgive others' wrongs against them until a new system of justice can be established.

In this section, we also gain a better understanding of Guenever. Until now we have seen her as more of a target for Lancelot's affections than an individual in her own right, and the portrait of her had previously been more flattering. In these chapters, however, Guenever begins to seem like a furtive, jealous, and secretive woman. She fears Arthur's retribution if he finds out about her affair, but she nonetheless continues the affair even after Lancelot tries to call it off. As her behavior worsens, so does her physical appearance, and she begins to use makeup to try to keep Lancelot attracted to her. The image of Guenever putting on makeup to cover her age suggests that she is trying to hide her true, immoral self. The narrator tries to temper such an unattractive picture of Guenever by telling us that Arthur is ten years older than she and that their marriage was arranged. With this qualifying description, we sympathize more with Guenever's situation, though we still do not applaud her lack of morals and honor.

The other major development in these chapters is Lancelot's newfound humility and piety. His failed quest for the Holy Grail has taught him that there are some goals that cannot be accomplished through skill in battle. Lancelot's son, Galahad, comes to exemplify this new knightly ideal instead. Since he is pure, pious, and virginal, only Galahad is able to accomplish the quest for the Holy Grail. Even though Galahad is the product of a union that was corrupt and dishonorable, he rises to become a highly moral figure. White, however, is more interested in humanity than in heroism, and he keeps Galahad as a minor character while Lancelot remains a pivotal figure. Like Malory, White is principally interested in the tragic aspects of King Arthur's story and in the circumstance that bring about the demise of Camelot and England's golden age. Galahad seems fairly cold, and almost inhuman, in his perfection. Lancelot, on the other hand, realizes his own mortality and his human failings, and sees that he can never reach the sterile perfection of his son. Lancelot's understanding of the limitations of his character demonstrates his maturity and humanness.

Book III: "The Ill-Made Knight," Chapters 38–45

Summary: Chapter 38

The day after Lancelot defends Guenever's honor, Nimue arrives and confirms that Guenever is innocent of poisoning the knight who died. This announcement comes as part of her promise to Merlyn to look after Arthur. Arthur decides to hold a tournament to celebrate Guenever's acquittal.

SUMMARY: CHAPTER 39

Lancelot visits Elaine, who tells him that he must now stay with her. He agrees to wear her favor, a red sleeve, on his helmet during the tournament. Lancelot fights valiantly, but is wounded near the end of the tournament when three knights attack him at once. When Guenever hears about Elaine's favor, she becomes jealous and angry, convinced that Lancelot loves Elaine.

SUMMARY: CHAPTER 40

When Lancelot returns to Camelot, he and Guenever fight. Finally aware that Lancelot does not love her and will never return to her, Elaine commits suicide. Her body is put in a barge, which drifts down to Camelot for all to see. At the sight of her dead rival, Guenever is filled with pity.

SUMMARY: CHAPTER 41

At another tournament soon after Elaine's suicide, the lines between the Round Table's factions become clear. Arthur sides against Lancelot for the first time, and Gareth sides with Lancelot against his own brothers. One day, Lancelot and Arthur hear that Guenever has been captured by a knight named Sir Meliagrance who has secretly been in love with her.

SUMMARY: CHAPTER 42

Meliagrance sets an ambush for Lancelot, but Lancelot manages to get through it and into the castle where Guenever is held captive. Meliagrance, knowing he will lose any battle with Lancelot, gives up and begs Guenever to forgive him. Lancelot consents to Guenever's request not to kill Meliagrance.

SUMMARY: CHAPTER 43

That night, Lancelot cuts through the bars of the window of Guenever's room, and the two sleep together for the first time in a long while. Lancelot cuts his hand as he breaks into her room. The next morning, Meliagrance discovers Lancelot's blood on Guenever's bed and accuses her of sleeping with one of the knights who guard her chamber, many of whom were wounded when she was kidnapped. Guenever denies the accusation. Her denial is accurate, since Lancelot is not one of the knights guarding her chamber. Lancelot offers to defend Guenever's honor in combat. Meliagrance, knowing he is no match for Lancelot, traps him in a dungeon in his castle.

SUMMARY: CHAPTER 44

Lancelot manages to persuade the girl who serves his meals to help him, and he escapes Meliagrance's dungeon and shows up for the challenge. Lancelot knocks Meliagrance off his horse in their first joust. Meliagrance begs for mercy. Lancelot looks to Guenever, who indicates that Meliagrance should be killed. Although the crowd agrees with Guenever, Lancelot does not kill Meliagrance outright. Instead, he handicaps himself by removing half his armor and tying his left hand behind his back. He then fights Meliagrance again and wins easily, cutting Meliagrance's head in half.

SUMMARY: CHAPTER 45

After the incident with Meliagrance, Camelot seems to be at peace again. Lancelot and Guenever are happy together, and Arthur does his best to ignore their affair. A man named Sir Urre, who has been cursed with wounds that will not heal, comes to Camelot in the hope that the best knight in the world will be able to heal him. All the knights place their hands on him, but to no avail. Finally Lancelot, who has been hiding in his room, afraid of failure, lays his hands on the man and cures him. The room bursts into a frenzy of celebration, except for Lancelot, who cries to himself like a child who has been beaten.

ANALYSIS: CHAPTERS 38–45

A lot occurs in these short, transitional chapters, but we get the sense that these are only loose ends being wrapped up before the story comes to its conclusion. Whereas "The Queen of Air and Darkness" ends with the disastrous liaison of Morgause and Arthur, "The Ill-Made Knight" concludes somewhat happily. The book ends with a burst of jubilation, and Camelot feels like a place of uneasy but real peace. After the chaos of the Holy Grail period, Camelot returns to the status quo. Certain story lines are brought to a close, and some secondary figures make their final exits. For example, Elaine commits suicide and thus no longer interferes with Lancelot's relationship with Guenever, eliminating a source of tension in Lancelot's and Guenever's lives.

The tone of these last chapters, however, feels almost sad, and even the greatest deeds are tainted. Lancelot is finally able to perform a miracle as the best knight in the world, but he does so in spite of his sins, not because of his accomplishments. Guenever is acquitted on a technicality of committing adultery with one of her knights.

Her honor is defended, but only because her champion proves to be stronger than her accuser. The three main characters, despite their sins, are able to remain in their roles, but only because they become resigned to the lie they live. The optimistic sense that things will resolve themselves is gone. When Lancelot heals Sir Urre, he cries because it seems to him that even miracles have lost their sincerity. Lancelot is not perfect, and the fact the he is allowed to perform miracles despite his sinfulness makes the whole endeavor seem cheap to him.

In these chapters we see also that Lancelot is a man who is fundamentally torn. He is both humble and proud, both ambitious and self-loathing, and he feels that his love for Arthur, Guenever, and God are in conflict. These contradictory impulses force him to lie to his best friend, kill a man for rightfully accusing his mistress of adultery, and ignore the mother of his only son. Lancelot is so afraid of his own failure that he hides in his room instead of trying to heal the man who needs his help. He expresses confidence and power to the world even though he feels insecure and unworthy inside. Despite all of his sins and despite his inner lack of confidence, Lancelot is still able to perform a miracle and cure a man who is mortally wounded. But he can save only others and is so steeped in sin that he feels he can no longer save himself.

Book IV: "The Candle in the Wind," Chapters 1–6

Summary: Chapter 1

Much time has passed. Agravaine is now fifty-five years old, fat and a borderline alcoholic. Mordred hates Arthur because he believes that Arthur abandoned him to die as an infant and because of the long-running feud between his mother's family and Arthur's. Agravaine hates Lancelot because Lancelot has defeated him in jousts countless times. They decide that the best way to get revenge on Arthur and Lancelot is to make Lancelot's affair with Guenever known to Arthur. Arthur will then have to prosecute Lancelot under the new system of laws he is trying to establish, and they will then destroy each other.

Summary: Chapter 2

Gawaine, Gaheris, and Gareth enter the room. When Gawaine finds out about Mordred and Agravaine's plot, he forbids them to go through with it. Mordred refuses to follow his orders. Agravaine, still a coward, pulls his sword on his unarmed brother, and Gawaine goes into a rage. He is on the verge of killing Agravaine when Arthur walks in, smiling benevolently at all of them.

SUMMARY: CHAPTER 3

Lancelot and Guenever sit by a window in Arthur's castle. The narrator describes the new England that they see before them. Arthur's reign has put an end to the horrors of the past. There is a burgeoning of artistic accomplishment, and different kinds of people mingle on the city streets.

SUMMARY: CHAPTER 4

Lancelot tells Guenever that Arthur knows all about their affair and will not punish them, but Guenever says they must be careful nonetheless. Lancelot is troubled because he loves Arthur too much to hurt him, but loves Guenever too much to leave her. Arthur steps into the door and hears them talking, but he quietly disappears to get a page to announce his presence. When Arthur returns, he, Lancelot, and Guenever have an awkward conversation about the Orkney family. Arthur tells them that Mordred is his son. He tells them too that he had heard horrible prophesies about Mordred and tried to kill him. Arthur, who was only nineteen at the time, ordered that all the babies of a certain age be put out to sea, but somehow Mordred survived. Arthur regrets his decision now and warns that Mordred is out for revenge and for the throne and that Mordred might try to use Guenever or Lancelot against him. He informs them that if he catches either of them working against his kingdom, he will be forced to prosecute the offender as the law sees fit.

SUMMARY: CHAPTER 5

Arthur goes to the Justice Room to work on the new laws. Gawaine, Gareth, Gaheris, Agravaine, and Mordred are there when he arrives. Gawaine, Gareth, and Gaheris have been trying to persuade Agravaine and Mordred not to tell Arthur about Lancelot and Guenever's affair, but when Arthur arrives, they tell him anyway, insisting that the matter should be decided by the new jury laws and not by combat. They say that if they can produce proof of the adultery, then Arthur is legally bound to bring the matter to trial. They tell Arthur that they will try to capture Lancelot in Guenever's room while Arthur is away hunting. Arthur eventually consents to their plan, but hopes aloud that Lancelot will kill all of his accusers. He also tells Agravaine and Mordred that if their accusation cannot be proven, he will prosecute them to the fullest extent of the law.

SUMMARY: CHAPTER 6

The first night that Arthur is away, Lancelot prepares to go to Guenever's quarters. Gareth warns him that Mordred and Agravaine plan to trap him in her room, but Lancelot ignores his warning.

ANALYSIS: CHAPTERS 1–6

The fourth book of *The Once and Future King,* "The Candle in the Wind," chronicles the tragic end of King Arthur's reign, and therefore the tone is serious. There are a few playful moments, such as when Lancelot and Guenever sing a duet together, but a feeling that doom is imminent for Camelot overshadows any satirical or comical interactions. As the book opens, Mordred and Agravaine are plotting to put an end to Arthur's rule, indicating the central role of revenge in this book's plot.

In the first two books, Arthur and Lancelot are young, ambitious, idealistic, and innocent. By the fourth book, they have developed what White calls the "seventh sense," a world-weariness that is the product of mistakes, sins, compromises, and betrayals. In these chapters, we see the heavy effect of this weariness on the main characters. Lancelot, Guenever, and Arthur have all come to depend on each other so much that the only real solution—for one of them to leave the situation—is impossible. Their joint histories of dishonor and sin—Lancelot and Guenever's affair, Lancelot's pride, Guenever's jealousy, Arthur's early massacre of infants, and Arthur's unwillingness to take a stand on the affair—irrevocably bind them together. Now that Mordred and Agravaine have united, it seems necessary for Arthur, Guenever, and Lancelot to stick together, although this inevitably makes things worse. The destruction of Camelot and the end of King Arthur's reign are now inevitable.

White's description of Arthur's character is compelling because Arthur's actions are so confusing and the right path so obscure. It is difficult to understand, for example, why Arthur does not warn Guenever and Lancelot that Mordred and Agravaine are setting a trap for them. Part of the explanation for Arthur's behavior is that he is still in denial of the affair, not willing to admit that he knows of it. The other explanation is that if Arthur were to warn Lancelot and Guenever, Arthur would be undermining his new system of justice. By warning them, Arthur would be helping them escape prosecution and would make himself their accomplice. Arthur's laws are the culmination of his conversations with Merlyn about the use of might and right; to abandon his faith in these laws would be to reject everything for which he stands. Mordred and Agravaine are aware of Arthur's commitment to justice, so they are able to trap him by his own rules and laws. Arthur does not want to unravel the society he has built, but to preserve it, he must sacrifice the two people he loves most.

Gareth's decision, in Chapter 6, to warn Lancelot about Mordred's plot is a stunning break with the Orkney faction and strong statement of loyalty to Lancelot. It is a sign both of Gareth's decency and of the respect that Lancelot has earned over the years. Lancelot's decision to ignore Gareth's advice, on the other hand, is a reminder of his pride. Despite his humiliation in the search for the Holy Grail, Lancelot still arrogantly assumes he knows what Arthur is capable of. Lancelot's brash faith in Arthur becomes more presumptuous than touching and has disastrous results.

BOOK IV: "THE CANDLE IN THE WIND," CHAPTERS 7–14

SUMMARY: CHAPTER 7

Lancelot and Guenever have a few tender moments before Guenever starts to fear that someone will discover them. Just as she is pushing Lancelot toward the door, they see that someone is trying to free the lock. Mordred, Agravaine, and twelve other fully armed knights are waiting outside the door. Lancelot manages to kill Agravaine and steal his sword and armor. He exchanges rings with Guenever and steps outside to face his enemies.

SUMMARY: CHAPTER 8

A week later, Gareth, Gawaine, Gaheris, and Mordred are sitting in the Justice Room. Mordred is criticized for running away from Lancelot, who slew all of the other knights outside of Guenever's chamber. Lancelot has since escaped back to his castle. Guenever has been convicted of adultery and is to be burned at the stake. Everyone expects Lancelot to rescue her. Arthur, at Mordred's urging, asks Gareth and Gaheris to join the guards who are already posted around her. They go unwillingly, without their armor. Just as Guenever is about to be burned, Lancelot and his knights arrive and rescue her. Arthur and Gawaine are both elated, and Arthur begins to plan out how their parties can be reconciled. Mordred returns from the scene and tells them that Lancelot killed Gareth and Gaheris, even though they were both unarmed. Neither Arthur nor Gawaine believes Mordred at first. Gawaine goes to confirm the news and returns heartbroken after finding Gareth and Gaheris dead.

SUMMARY: CHAPTER 9

Six months later, Lancelot and Guenever are in Lancelot's castle, called Joyous Gard, which is under siege. Lancelot tells Guenever that he does not remember killing Gareth and Gaheris, but that he may well have done so in the confusion. Guenever decides that the only way to save themselves, and Arthur, is to ask the Church to intervene.

SUMMARY: CHAPTER 10

The Church agrees to mediate a peace. Back in Camelot, the bishop of Rochester presides over the decision. Lancelot is banished from England, and Guenever returns to Arthur. Gawaine swears, however, that he will still try to get his revenge on Lancelot.

SUMMARY: CHAPTER 11

Arthur and Gawaine follow Lancelot to France and place one of his castles under siege. Back in England, Guenever and her maid Agnes are knitting together in her chambers when Mordred enters. He is now quite mad, excessively dandy, and consumed by cruelty. He has founded a new political order, called the Thrashers, who speak of the old Gaelic wars and want to massacre Jews. Mordred tells Guenever that he plans to announce that Arthur and Gawaine have been killed in France and that he is the new king of England. Mordred also tells Guenever that he intends to take her as his wife.

SUMMARY: CHAPTER 12

In Arthur's tent on the battlefield in France, Gawaine is trying to recover from a blow he receives during a fight with Lancelot. It is the second time Lancelot has defeated Gawaine and the second time Lancelot has chosen not to kill him. The bishop of Rochester enters with a letter from Guenever. It tells Arthur about Mordred's plot. Arthur decides to lift the siege and return to England immediately. Gawaine, who is badly injured, insists on going as well, anxious to wreak revenge on his treacherous brother.

SUMMARY: CHAPTER 13

In his castle, Lancelot has just received a letter from Gawaine, who is now in England, telling him what Mordred has done. Gawaine writes that Guenever and her allies are defending themselves in the Tower of London, which Mordred is attacking with cannons. Gawaine forgives Lancelot for killing Gareth and Gaheris and asks him to return to England to help Arthur. He adds that his wound from Lancelot has reopened in battle and that he has been "hurt to the death." Lancelot and his comrades decide to return to England at once.

SUMMARY: CHAPTER 14

Arthur is in his pavilion on the battlefield at Kent, where his forces are fighting Mordred's army. It is late at night and he is working on his laws. Arthur begins to think about the reasons for war and what can be done to stop it from occurring. He calls for a page named Thomas Malory and tells him that Malory must remember the story of King Arthur, particularly the idea that might must be used for right. Arthur asks Malory to spread Arthur's message of justice and peace. Malory agrees to do so, and after Malory leaves, Arthur begins to cry. He thinks of the lessons he learned from the animals when he was a young boy. He wakes up with a fresh mind, hopeful for the day when his dream will be fulfilled. He stands up and prepares himself for his final battle.

ANALYSIS: CHAPTERS 7–14

In this section, the delicate relationships between Arthur, Guenever, Lancelot, and the Orkney faction quickly unravel. The first step in the final destruction of Camelot is Mordred and Agravaine's discovery of Lancelot in Guenever's room. Although Lancelot saves himself from being killed, he has promised Arthur that he will not kill Mordred, and he is forced to leave one witness alive. Mordred then accuses Guenever of adultery. Arthur must follow his own laws and honor the accusation. Arthur's deeply ambivalent feelings about the situation are reflected in his unwillingness to take any personal action to save Guenever and in his fervent hope that Lancelot will rescue her. The second step in the collapse of Arthur's reign is Lancelot's accidental killing of Gareth and Gaheris. Since the only account of their deaths comes from Mordred, we are never sure that Lancelot is their killer. Lancelot does not think he killed the two men, but he lies about why he was in Guenever's room, and thus we cannot be certain that he is not simply concealing an evil deed. The ambiguity of Lancelot's guilt makes Arthur's position even more difficult. He cannot be sure that his best friend is guilty of killing Gareth and Gaheris, but he has to take decisive action against him.

The tone and pacing of the narrative in these last chapters differs from the tone and pace of the narrative in the earlier books of *The Once and Future King*. Unlike the slow, satirical, and sometimes frivolous description of the Wart's childhood in Book I, or the fast-paced action scenes of Lancelot's numerous quests and battles in Book III, the narrative in Book IV is jumpy, episodic, subtle, ominous, and mysterious. White constantly switches the narrative from one conversation to another, and we learn about events from a wide variety of perspectives. For example, we hear about Gawaine's battles with Lancelot and Guenever's flight from Mordred after they occur. White shapes the narrative in this way for a reason: the final book is extremely short, but its plot is complicated, so there is not enough space for the kinds of descriptions that we find in Book III. The length of the book is not the only reason for its choppy, fragmented style, however. Another reason is that the story is no longer trying to sidestep the issue of Camelot's demise, since its downfall is now imminent and unavoidable. Instead, the novel describes what is left of Arthur's empire in a manner that reflects how fragmented the kingdom has become.

Important Quotations Explained

1. Power is of the individual mind, but the mind's power is not enough. Power of the body decides everything in the end, and only Might is Right.

The great pike, king of the fish in Sir Ector's moat, speaks these words to the Wart in Book I, Chapter 5, after Merlyn transforms the Wart into a fish. The great pike presents a simplistic view of power and the nature of leadership. He insists that power is a value in itself, to be sought and exercised for its own sake and instituted by physical force. The Wart's discussion with the pike is his first exposure to a philosophy of government that emphasizes force. The Wart responds to the pike's views with disgust, which suggests that he has the potential to be a just, good ruler. This quote is also important because it presents the vocabulary of power and morality that will dominate Arthur's mind for the rest of his life. He begins to consider the relationship between "Might" and "Right," and to criticize the status quo of English society. Arthur's firsthand experience with the pike's style of leadership motivates him to be a different type of ruler and to formulate a new type of philosophy about war and justice.

2.   Why can't you harness Might so that it works for Right?…
      The Might is there, in the bad half of people, and you can't
      neglect it.

Arthur utters these words in a speech from Book II, Chapter 6, in
which he first articulates the philosophy that is to make him such a
great ruler. He synthesizes the lessons he has learned from Merlyn
and decides to use his new position of king to harness physical force
to establish morality. He expresses his belief that the proper function of power is to subordinate might to right. This idea may seem
simplistic to modern readers, but White presents a medieval world
in which force is blindly equated with justice and shows that it is
truly innovative for Arthur to draw a distinction between power
and justice. Essentially, White shows that Arthur is a king worth
remembering not for his heroism or his military exploits, but because he champions the idea of civilized society. He recognizes that
all people have a good side and a bad side and thinks his political
philosophy will allow him to harness people's bad sides for the common good. For example, knights who long to fight will still be able
to fight, but they will fight against those who do evil deeds rather
than fight for its own sake.

3.   It is why Sir Thomas Malory called his very long book
      the Death of Arthur. . . . It is the tragedy . . . of sin coming
      home to roost. . . . [W]e have to take note of the parentage
      of Arthur's son Mordred, and to remember . . . that the
      king had slept with his own sister. He did not know he was
      doing so . . . but it seems, in tragedy, that innocence is not
      enough.

This passage, from Book II, Chapter 14, closes the second book of
the novel and introduces a dark tone that carries over into Book III.
Immediately before these lines, White presents Mordred's family
tree and reveals that Morgause, the woman Arthur has just slept
with, is in fact his half-sister. White locates the downfall of Arthur's
reign in this one unwitting sin. White suggests that it is this evil
deed that begins Arthur's downfall and tragedy. Arthur's sins come
"home to roost" in the vengeful Mordred, who is the result of the
incestuous union between Arthur and Morgause. This passage suggests the evil within Mordred's character and foreshadows his role
in precipitating the fall of Camelot and Arthur. This quote is important because it offers White's personal analysis of the Arthur saga
and exemplifies White's frequent allusions to Malory as the definitive teller of the Arthurian legend.

QUOTATIONS

4.   [H]e had a contradictory nature which was far from
      holy. . . For one thing, he liked to hurt people.

This description of Lancelot comes from Book III, Chapter 6. White
describes the inner conflict that drives Lancelot—namely, a commitment to holiness that develops because of his inclination to be cruel.
White explains how the clash between Lancelot's good and bad
selves leads to his heroic behavior. Lancelot has some terrible characteristics, including cruelty and a love of violence, but he is committed to his desire to be honorable. Thus, he transforms his hidden
insecurities and guilt into an outward drive to commit good deeds
and heroic acts. White explains that Lancelot is a merciful warrior
not despite his cruelty but because of it. Whereas a knight like Gawaine has no problem ending a vanquished enemy's life, Lancelot
views such an unmerciful deed as caving in to his despicable side.
Lancelot's deep self-hatred causes him to act gently and nobly when-
ever he can, since he wants to deprive himself of the pleasure that
cruelty gives him. If Lancelot did not want so badly to be cruel, he
would not act so mercifully. This paradoxical arrangement is typical
of Lancelot's conflicted personality, which causes him intense suf-
fering. White calls Lancelot a "poor fellow" and an ill-made knight
because of his inability to handle this inner conflict.

QUOTATIONS

5.   It was in the nature of [Arthur's] bold mind to hope, in
      these circumstances, that he would not find [Lancelot and
      Guenever] together. . . . [H]e was hoping to weather the
      trouble by refusing to become conscious of it.

This passage from Book III, Chapter 16 describes Arthur's attitude
toward the love affair between Lancelot and Guenever. In the end,
Arthur's complacency in these early stages of the affair leads to
his downfall, as he is forced to put a stop to the affair after it has
gone too far. This quotation describes Arthur's simpleminded yet
optimistic reaction to his unconscious suspicion that Lancelot and
Guenever have betrayed him. Arthur suppresses his fears because he
loves and trusts them both. Once he accepts that the people he loves
have sinned against him, he chooses to ignore their sin to preserve
their love. Arthur's self-sacrifice is typical of his behavior, and is
one of the qualities that makes him a sympathetic character rather
than merely a pathetic one. Arthur is not fooled by Lancelot and
Guenever's lies, but he makes a deliberate choice not to see through
them, so as to protect his loved ones' happiness. Society would consider his wife's adultery treason and call for Guenever and Lancelot
to be executed, so Arthur sacrifices his own happiness to cover up
their betrayal and save their lives.

QUOTATIONS

KEY FACTS

FULL TITLE
The Once and Future King

AUTHOR
T. H. (Terence Hanbury) White

TYPE OF WORK
Novel

GENRE
Fantasy; heroic epic; satire

LANGUAGE
English

TIME AND PLACE WRITTEN
England; 1936–1958

DATE OF FIRST PUBLICATION
1958. The four books that make up the novel were previously
published separately: "The Sword in the Stone" in 1938; "The
Queen of Air and Darkness" (published as *The Witch in the
Wood*) in 1939; "The Ill-Made Knight" in 1940; and "The
Candle in the Wind" in 1958.

PUBLISHER
G. P. Putnam's Sons

NARRATOR
The narrator speaks in the third person and is omniscient, or
all-knowing. The narrator has access to the thoughts of all
the characters and provides commentary on the context of the
work, as in the references to Adolf Hitler, Uncle Sam, and Sir
Thomas Malory.

POINT OF VIEW
In general, the novel oscillates among the points of view of
Arthur, Lancelot, and Guenever, though it occasionally assumes
the point of view of minor characters such as Elaine and
Gawaine.

TONE
>   The tone changes throughout the four books of the novel. It is playful and satirical in the first book, but gradually grows darker and more serious

TENSE
>   Past

SETTING (TIME)
>   The era of King Arthur, a legendary figure in the folklore of medieval England

SETTING (PLACE)
>   Medieval England and France

PROTAGONIST
>   Arthur, who is called the Wart in Book I, is the protagonist of most of the novel, but Lancelot is the protagonist of the third book.

MAJOR CONFLICT
>   Arthur struggles to transform feudal England into a civilized country in which strength does not overwhelm justice.

RISING ACTION
>   Lancelot's destructive love affair with Guenever; the jealous conspiracies of the Orkney faction; Arthur's incestuous affair with Morgause

CLIMAX
>   Because the novel is episodic in form, each of its books comes to its own minor climax: in Book I, Arthur's becoming king; in Book II, Morgause's seduction of Arthur; in Book III, the blossoming of Lancelot and Guenever's affair; and in Book IV, the exposing of Lancelot and Guenever's affair.

FALLING ACTION
>   Arthur wages war against Lancelot; Mordred seizes power in England

THEMES
>   The relationship between force and justice; the senselessness of war; the frivolity of knighthood

MOTIFS
>   Myths and legends; blood sports; castles

KEY FACTS

SYMBOLS

The Round Table; the Questing Beast; the Holy Grail

FORESHADOWING

Merlyn's frequent comments about Arthur's future and death hint at the destruction of Camelot and the demise of Arthur's reign, which is the most prominent subject of foreshadowing in the novel.

STUDY QUESTIONS

1. *The tone of Book I is drastically different from the tone of Book IV. Book I is lighthearted and leisurely, whereas Book IV is tragic and fast paced. In your view, how do these two books come together? Which themes and elements of style connect them?*

The two books between the Book I and Book IV provide a bridge from the lightheartedness of the Wart's adventures in the Forest Sauvage to King Arthur's final despair. This transition is enormous but gradual. In Book II, the world of Orkney is grim, but this grimness is offset by the antics of Sir Pellinore, Sir Grummore, and Sir Palomides. In Book III, the tone becomes darker, but the book also has a triumphant tone during the narration of Lancelot's adventures.

While the tone drastically changes from Book I to Book IV, the themes and ideas expressed in these two books are similar. King Arthur, a simpleminded and optimistic man in Book IV, still has the childhood naïveté he shows in Book I. Also, the frivolity of knighthood appears in the first and last books. For example, King Pellinore's refusal to kill his beloved Questing Beast is as pointless and silly a gesture as the trials by combat that appear in the fourth book. White also continues to point to the future in both books with his insinuations that Arthur's reign will not last.

2.   *The quest for the Holy Grail is a central part of the*
       Arthurian legend, but it gets only seven short chapters
       in Book III of THE ONCE AND FUTURE KING. *What is*
       the relevance of the quest to the idea of might versus
       right?

The quest for the Holy Grail is Arthur's attempt to get his knights to use their aggression productively. Once the knights have no more good deeds or chivalric acts to perform, they do not know what to do with their power. Arthur wants the restless knights to fight for a noble cause and therefore assigns them to fight for God. The quest is successful in that it occupies the knights for some time and even achieves its goal when the pious Sir Galahad finds the Holy Grail. The quest for the Holy Grail, however, has disastrous effects on Arthur's court. Half of the knights are killed during the quest, and those who succeed on the quest disappear because they have reached perfection. The few knights who return unharmed do not seem to have learned anything from their adventure and are upset over the loss of their comrades. After the quest, the surviving knights are still just as bloodthirsty as they were when they started the quest, and they are certainly no holier or closer to God.

White does not focus on the quest for the Holy Grail in his novel in part because it is a detour in Arthur's progress toward justice as the basis of civilization. Like Arthur's attempt to use war on behalf of justice, the quest for the Holy Grail is his attempt to use war to serve God. Only later does Arthur realize that this goal asks too much, since it requires people to abandon their bad side instead of using it productively.

3.   *Most of Arthur's conclusions about might and right*
     come from Merlyn. To what extent do you think
     Arthur learns to think for himself by the end of the
     novel and to what extent is he simply still repeating
     what Merlyn has taught him?

The end of the novel describes Arthur's personal beliefs and individual thoughts about war and justice, one of the few times that White lets us see what Arthur is thinking. For the most part, even in Book I, Arthur's inner needs, thoughts, and concerns remain mysterious, and it is hard to gauge his commitment to his principles. Throughout the novel, we hear him repeat Merlyn's ideas and beliefs about government and power, and once Nimue captures Merlyn, Arthur's beliefs no longer develop. It would appear that Arthur is unable to generate ideas without the help of his mentor, but in Book IV, Arthur does arrive at some original conclusions. For example, he concludes that national boundaries are the source of conflicts and that if they could be abolished, war would disappear as well. This idea about the nature of conflict seems to be his own, which suggests that Arthur does finally learn to think for himself. Unfortunately, however, Arthur's timing is poor. Now that he has developed his own ideas, he will die the next day. Even if he were not to die, he would still be too powerless to implement any of his ideas. The futility of his situation undermines the significance of his last thoughts.

STUDY QUESTIONS

How to Write Literary Analysis

The Literary Essay: A Step-by-Step Guide

When you read for pleasure, your only goal is enjoyment. You might find yourself reading to get caught up in an exciting story, to learn about an interesting time or place, or just to pass time. Maybe you're looking for inspiration, guidance, or a reflection of your own life. There are as many different, valid ways of reading a book as there are books in the world.

When you read a work of literature in an English class, however, you're being asked to read in a special way: you're being asked to perform *literary analysis*. To analyze something means to break it down into smaller parts and then examine how those parts work, both individually and together. Literary analysis involves examining all the parts of a novel, play, short story, or poem—elements such as character, setting, tone, and imagery—and thinking about how the author uses those elements to create certain effects.

A literary essay isn't a book review: you're not being asked whether or not you liked a book or whether you'd recommend it to another reader. A literary essay also isn't like the kind of book report you wrote when you were younger, where your teacher wanted you to summarize the book's action. A high school- or college-level literary essay asks, "How does this piece of literature actually work?" "How does it do what it does?" and, "Why might the author have made the choices he or she did?"

The Seven Steps

No one is born knowing how to analyze literature; it's a skill you learn and a process you can master. As you gain more practice with this kind of thinking and writing, you'll be able to craft a method that works best for you. But until then, here are seven basic steps to writing a well-constructed literary essay:

1. *Ask questions*
2. *Collect evidence*
3. *Construct a thesis*

4. *Develop and organize arguments*
5. *Write the introduction*
6. *Write the body paragraphs*
7. *Write the conclusion*

---

1. ASK QUESTIONS

When you're assigned a literary essay in class, your teacher will often provide you with a list of writing prompts. Lucky you! Now all you have to do is choose one. Do yourself a favor and pick a topic that interests you. You'll have a much better (not to mention easier) time if you start off with something you enjoy thinking about. If you are asked to come up with a topic by yourself, though, you might start to feel a little panicked. Maybe you have too many ideas—or none at all. Don't worry. Take a deep breath and start by asking yourself these questions:

- **What struck you?** Did a particular image, line, or scene linger in your mind for a long time? If it fascinated you, chances are you can draw on it to write a fascinating essay.

- **What confused you?** Maybe you were surprised to see a character act in a certain way, or maybe you didn't understand why the book ended the way it did. Confusing moments in a work of literature are like a loose thread in a sweater: if you pull on it, you can unravel the entire thing. Ask yourself why the author chose to write about that character or scene the way he or she did and you might tap into some important insights about the work as a whole.

- **Did you notice any patterns?** Is there a phrase that the main character uses constantly or an image that repeats throughout the book? If you can figure out how that pattern weaves through the work and what the significance of that pattern is, you've almost got your entire essay mapped out.

- **Did you notice any contradictions or ironies?** Great works of literature are complex; great literary essays recognize and explain those complexities. Maybe the title (*Happy Days*) totally disagrees with the book's subject matter (hungry orphans dying in the woods). Maybe the main character acts one way around his family and a completely different way around his friends and associates. If you can find a way to explain a work's contradictory elements, you've got the seeds of a great essay.

At this point, you don't need to know exactly what you're going to say about your topic; you just need a place to begin your exploration. You can help direct your reading and brainstorming by formulating your topic as a *question*, which you'll then try to answer in your essay. The best questions invite critical debates and discussions, not just a rehashing of the summary. Remember, you're looking for something you can *prove or argue* based on evidence you find in the text. Finally, remember to keep the scope of your question in mind: is this a topic you can adequately address within the word or page limit you've been given? Conversely, is this a topic big enough to fill the required length?

Good Questions

"Are Romeo and Juliet's parents responsible for the deaths of their children?"

"Why do pigs keep showing up in Lord of the Flies?*"*

"Are Dr. Frankenstein and his monster alike? How?"

Bad Questions

"What happens to Scout in To Kill a Mockingbird?*"*

"What do the other characters in Julius Caesar *think about Caesar?"*

"How does Hester Prynne in The Scarlet Letter *remind me of my sister?"*

---

2. Collect Evidence

Once you know what question you want to answer, it's time to scour the book for things that will help you answer the question. Don't worry if you don't know what you want to say yet—right now you're just collecting ideas and material and letting it all percolate. Keep track of passages, symbols, images, or scenes that deal with your topic. Eventually, you'll start making connections between these examples and your thesis will emerge.

Here's a brief summary of the various parts that compose each and every work of literature. These are the elements that you will analyze in your essay, and which you will offer as evidence to support your arguments. For more on the parts of literary works, see the Glossary of Literary Terms at the end of this section.

LITERARY ANALYSIS

ELEMENTS OF STORY   These are the *what*s of the work—what happens, where it happens, and to whom it happens.

- **Plot:** All of the events and actions of the work.

- **Character:** The people who act and are acted upon in a literary work. The main character of a work is known as the *protagonist.*

- **Conflict:** The central tension in the work. In most cases, the protagonist wants something, while opposing forces (antagonists) hinder the protagonist's progress.

- **Setting:** When and where the work takes place. Elements of setting include location, time period, time of day, weather, social atmosphere, and economic conditions.

- **Narrator:** The person telling the story. The narrator may straightforwardly report what happens, convey the subjective opinions and perceptions of one or more characters, or provide commentary and opinion in his or her own voice.

- **Themes:** The main idea or message of the work—usually an abstract idea about people, society, or life in general. A work may have many themes, which may be in tension with one another.

ELEMENTS OF STYLE   These are the *how*s—how the characters speak, how the story is constructed, and how language is used throughout the work.

- **Structure and organization:** How the parts of the work are assembled. Some novels are narrated in a linear, chronological fashion, while others skip around in time. Some plays follow a traditional three- or five-act structure, while others are a series of loosely connected scenes. Some authors deliberately leave gaps in their works, leaving readers to puzzle out the missing information. A work's structure and organization can tell you a lot about the kind of message it wants to convey.

- **Point of view:** The perspective from which a story is told. In *first-person point of view,* the narrator involves him or herself in the story. ("I went to the store"; "We watched in horror as the bird slammed into the window.") A first-person narrator is usually the protagonist of the work, but not always. In *third-person point of view,* the narrator does not participate in the story. A third-person narrator may closely follow a specific character, recounting that individual character's thoughts or experiences, or it may be what we call an *omniscient* narrator. Omniscient narrators see and know all: they can witness any event in any time or place and are privy to the inner thoughts and feelings of all characters. Remember that the narrator and the author are not the same thing!

- **Diction:** Word choice. Whether a character uses dry, clinical language or flowery prose with lots of exclamation points can tell you a lot about his or her attitude and personality.

- **Syntax:** Word order and sentence construction. Syntax is a crucial part of establishing an author's narrative voice. Ernest Hemingway, for example, is known for writing in very short, straightforward sentences, while James Joyce characteristically wrote in long, incredibly complicated lines.

- **Tone:** The mood or feeling of the text. Diction and syntax often contribute to the tone of a work. A novel written in short, clipped sentences that use small, simple words might feel brusque, cold, or matter-of-fact.

- **Imagery:** Language that appeals to the senses, representing things that can be seen, smelled, heard, tasted, or touched.

- **Figurative language:** Language that is not meant to be interpreted literally. The most common types of figurative language are *metaphors* and *similes,* which compare two unlike things in order to suggest a similarity between them— for example, "All the world's a stage," or "The moon is like a ball of green cheese." (Metaphors say one thing *is* another thing; similes claim that one thing is *like* another thing.)

---

3. CONSTRUCT A THESIS

When you've examined all the evidence you've collected and know how you want to answer the question, it's time to write your thesis statement. A *thesis* is a claim about a work of literature that needs to be supported by evidence and arguments. The thesis statement is the heart of the literary essay, and the bulk of your paper will be spent trying to prove this claim. A good thesis will be:

- **Arguable.** "*The Great Gatsby* describes New York society in the 1920s" isn't a thesis—it's a fact.

- **Provable through textual evidence**. "*Hamlet* is a confusing but ultimately very well-written play" is a weak thesis because it offers the writer's personal opinion about the book. Yes, it's arguable, but it's not a claim that can be proved or supported with examples taken from the play itself.

- **Surprising**. "Both George and Lenny change a great deal in *Of Mice and Men*" is a weak thesis because it's obvious. A really strong thesis will argue for a reading of the text that is not immediately apparent.

- **Specific**. "Dr. Frankenstein's monster tells us a lot about the human condition" is *almost* a really great thesis statement, but it's still too vague. What does the writer mean by "a lot"? *How* does the monster tell us so much about the human condition?

GOOD THESIS STATEMENTS

Question: In *Romeo and Juliet*, which is more powerful in shaping the lovers' story: fate or foolishness?

Thesis: "Though Shakespeare defines Romeo and Juliet as 'star-crossed lovers' and images of stars and planets appear throughout the play, a closer examination of that celestial imagery reveals that the stars are merely witnesses to the characters' foolish activities and not the causes themselves."

Question: How does the bell jar function as a symbol in Sylvia Plath's *The Bell Jar*?

Thesis: "A bell jar is a bell-shaped glass that has three basic uses: to hold a specimen for observation, to contain gases, and to maintain a vacuum. The bell jar appears in each of these capacities in *The Bell Jar*, Plath's semi-autobiographical novel, and each appearance marks a different stage in Esther's mental breakdown."

Question: Would Piggy in *The Lord of the Flies* make a good island leader if he were given the chance?

Thesis: "Though the intelligent, rational, and innovative Piggy has the mental characteristics of a good leader, he ultimately lacks the social skills necessary to be an effective one. Golding emphasizes this point by giving Piggy a foil in the charismatic Jack, whose magnetic personality allows him to capture and wield power effectively, if not always wisely."

4. DEVELOP AND ORGANIZE ARGUMENTS

The reasons and examples that support your thesis will form the middle paragraphs of your essay. Since you can't really write your thesis statement until you know how you'll structure your argument, you'll probably end up working on steps 3 and 4 at the same time.

There's no single method of argumentation that will work in every context. One essay prompt might ask you to compare and contrast two characters, while another asks you to trace an image through a given work of literature. These questions require different kinds of answers and therefore different kinds of arguments. Below, we'll discuss three common kinds of essay prompts and some strategies for constructing a solid, well-argued case.

TYPES OF LITERARY ESSAYS

- **Compare and contrast**

  Compare and contrast the characters of Huck and Jim in THE ADVENTURES OF HUCKLEBERRY FINN.

  Chances are you've written this kind of essay before. In an academic literary context, you'll organize your arguments the same way you would in any other class. You can either go *subject by subject* or *point by point*. In the former, you'll discuss one character first and then the second. In the latter, you'll choose several traits (attitude toward life, social status, images and metaphors associated with the character) and devote a paragraph to each. You may want to use a mix of these two approaches—for example, you may want to spend a paragraph apiece broadly sketching Huck's and Jim's personalities before transitioning into a paragraph or two that describes a few key points of comparison. This can be a highly effective strategy if you want to make a counterintuitive argument—that, despite seeming to be totally different, the two objects being compared are actually similar in a very important way (or vice versa). Remember that your essay should reveal something fresh or unexpected about the text, so think beyond the obvious parallels and differences.

- **Trace**

  Choose an image—for example, birds, knives, or eyes—and trace that image throughout MACBETH.

  Sounds pretty easy, right? All you need to do is read the play, underline every appearance of a knife in *Macbeth*, and then list

LITERARY ANALYSIS

them in your essay in the order they appear, right? Well, not exactly. Your teacher doesn't want a simple catalog of examples. He or she wants to see you make *connections* between those examples—that's the difference between summarizing and analyzing. In the *Macbeth* example above, think about the different contexts in which knives appear in the play and to what effect. In *Macbeth,* there are real knives and imagined knives; knives that kill and knives that simply threaten. Categorize and classify your examples to give them some order. Finally, always keep the overall effect in mind. After you choose and analyze your examples, you should come to some greater understanding about the work, as well as your chosen image, symbol, or phrase's role in developing the major themes and stylistic strategies of that work.

- **Debate**

    Is the society depicted in 1984 good for its citizens?

    In this kind of essay, you're being asked to debate a moral, ethical, or aesthetic issue regarding the work. You might be asked to judge a character or group of characters (*Is Caesar responsible for his own demise?*) or the work itself (*Is* JANE EYRE *a feminist novel?*). For this kind of essay, there are two important points to keep in mind. First, don't simply base your arguments on your personal feelings and reactions. Every literary essay expects you to read and analyze the work, so search for evidence in the text. What do characters in *1984* have to say about the government of Oceania? What images does Orwell use that might give you a hint about his attitude toward the government? As in any debate, you also need to make sure that you define all the necessary terms before you begin to argue your case. What does it mean to be a "good" society? What makes a novel "feminist"? You should define your terms right up front, in the first paragraph after your introduction.

    Second, remember that strong literary essays make contrary and surprising arguments. Try to think outside the box. In the *1984* example above, it seems like the obvious answer would be no, the totalitarian society depicted in Orwell's novel is *not* good for its citizens. But can you think of any arguments for the opposite side? Even if your final assertion is that the novel depicts a cruel, repressive, and therefore harmful society, acknowledging and responding to the counterargument will strengthen your overall case.

5. WRITE THE INTRODUCTION

Your introduction sets up the entire essay. It's where you present your topic and articulate the particular issues and questions you'll be addressing. It's also where you, as the writer, introduce yourself to your readers. A persuasive literary essay immediately establishes its writer as a knowledgeable, authoritative figure.

An introduction can vary in length depending on the overall length of the essay, but in a traditional five-paragraph essay it should be no longer than one paragraph. However long it is, your introduction needs to:

- **Provide any necessary context.** Your introduction should situate the reader and let him or her know what to expect. What book are you discussing? Which characters? What topic will you be addressing?

- **Answer the "So what?" question.** Why is this topic important, and why is your particular position on the topic noteworthy? Ideally, your introduction should pique the reader's interest by suggesting how your argument is surprising or otherwise counterintuitive. Literary essays make unexpected connections and reveal less-than-obvious truths.

- **Present your thesis.** This usually happens at or very near the end of your introduction.

- **Indicate the shape of the essay to come.** Your reader should finish reading your introduction with a good sense of the scope of your essay as well as the path you'll take toward proving your thesis. You don't need to spell out every step, but you do need to suggest the organizational pattern you'll be using.

Your introduction should not:

- **Be vague.** Beware of the two killer words in literary analysis: *interesting* and *important*. Of course the work, question, or example is interesting and important—that's why you're writing about it!

- **Open with any grandiose assertions.** Many student readers think that beginning their essays with a flamboyant statement such as, "Since the dawn of time, writers have been fascinated with the topic of free will," makes them sound important and commanding. You know what? It actually sounds pretty amateurish.

- **Wildly praise the work.** Another typical mistake student writers make is extolling the work or author. Your teacher doesn't need to be told that "Shakespeare is perhaps the greatest writer in the English language." You can mention a work's reputation in passing—by referring to *The Adventures of Huckleberry Finn* as "Mark Twain's enduring classic," for example—but don't make a point of bringing it up unless that reputation is key to your argument.

- **Go off-topic.** Keep your introduction streamlined and to the point. Don't feel the need to throw in all kinds of bells and whistles in order to impress your reader—just get to the point as quickly as you can, without skimping on any of the required steps.

---

6. Write the Body Paragraphs

Once you've written your introduction, you'll take the arguments you developed in step 4 and turn them into your body paragraphs. The organization of this middle section of your essay will largely be determined by the argumentative strategy you use, but no matter how you arrange your thoughts, your body paragraphs need to do the following:

- **Begin with a strong topic sentence.** Topic sentences are like signs on a highway: they tell the reader where they are and where they're going. A good topic sentence not only alerts readers to what issue will be discussed in the following paragraph but also gives them a sense of what argument will be made *about* that issue. "Rumor and gossip play an important role in *The Crucible*" isn't a strong topic sentence because it doesn't tell us very much. "The community's constant gossiping creates an environment that allows false accusations to flourish" is a much stronger topic sentence— it not only tells us *what* the paragraph will discuss (gossip) but *how* the paragraph will discuss the topic (by showing how gossip creates a set of conditions that leads to the play's climactic action).

- **Fully and completely develop a single thought.** Don't skip around in your paragraph or try to stuff in too much material. Body paragraphs are like bricks: each individual one needs to be strong and sturdy or the entire structure will collapse. Make sure you have really proven your point before moving on to the next one.

- **Use transitions effectively.** Good literary essay writers know that each paragraph must be clearly and strongly linked to the material around it. Think of each paragraph as a response to the one that precedes it. Use transition words and phrases such as *however, similarly, on the contrary, therefore,* and *furthermore* to indicate what kind of response you're making.

---

7. WRITE THE CONCLUSION

Just as you used the introduction to ground your readers in the topic before providing your thesis, you'll use the conclusion to quickly summarize the specifics learned thus far and then hint at the broader implications of your topic. A good conclusion will:

- **Do more than simply restate the thesis.** If your thesis argued that *The Catcher in the Rye* can be read as a Christian allegory, don't simply end your essay by saying, "And that is why *The Catcher in the Rye* can be read as a Christian allegory." If you've constructed your arguments well, this kind of statement will just be redundant.

- **Synthesize the arguments, not summarize them.** Similarly, don't repeat the details of your body paragraphs in your conclusion. The reader has already read your essay, and chances are it's not so long that they've forgotten all your points by now.

- **Revisit the "So what?" question.** In your introduction, you made a case for why your topic and position are important. You should close your essay with the same sort of gesture. What do your readers know now that they didn't know before? How will that knowledge help them better appreciate or understand the work overall?

- **Move from the specific to the general.** Your essay has most likely treated a very specific element of the work—a single character, a small set of images, or a particular passage. In your conclusion, try to show how this narrow discussion has wider implications for the work overall. If your essay on *To Kill a Mockingbird* focused on the character of Boo Radley, for example, you might want to include a bit in your conclusion about how he fits into the novel's larger message about childhood, innocence, or family life.

- **Stay relevant.** Your conclusion should suggest new directions of thought, but it shouldn't be treated as an opportunity to pad your essay with all the extra, interesting ideas you came up with during your brainstorming sessions but couldn't fit into the essay proper. Don't attempt to stuff in unrelated queries or too many abstract thoughts.

- **Avoid making overblown closing statements.** A conclusion should open up your highly specific, focused discussion, but it should do so without drawing a sweeping lesson about life or human nature. Making such observations may be part of the point of reading, but it's almost always a mistake in essays, where these observations tend to sound overly dramatic or simply silly.

A+ ESSAY CHECKLIST

Congratulations! If you've followed all the steps we've outlined above, you should have a solid literary essay to show for all your efforts. What if you've got your sights set on an A+? To write the kind of superlative essay that will be rewarded with a perfect grade, keep the following rubric in mind. These are the qualities that teachers expect to see in a truly A+ essay. How does yours stack up?

- ✓ Demonstrates a thorough understanding of the book
- ✓ Presents an original, compelling argument
- ✓ Thoughtfully analyzes the text's formal elements
- ✓ Uses appropriate and insightful examples
- ✓ Structures ideas in a logical and progressive order
- ✓ Demonstrates a mastery of sentence construction, transitions, grammar, spelling, and word choice

Suggested Essay Topics

1. Lancelot is a complex character, torn between cruelty and compassion. Discuss how such conflicts affect Lancelot's relationships with Guenever, Arthur, God, and chivalry.

2. The Wart has numerous adventures when Merlyn changes him into the form of animals, but only five of them are described in detail: his transformations into a perch, a merlin, a badger, an ant, and a goose. Briefly discuss the relevance each of these episodes has to the idea of might versus right and the development of Arthur's thoughts about civilization and government.

3. White wrote THE ONCE AND FUTURE KING in the form of numerous short, episodic chapters. Discuss the effect of this format on the pacing, plot, and character development of the novel.

4. The novel generally presents an antiwar message, but nevertheless draws a great deal of dramatic power from the conflict inherent in warfare. Is the novel's attitude toward war consistent, or does White contradict himself by glorifying battles?

A+ STUDENT ESSAY

> Contrast the episode of the ants with the episode of the
> geese. How does the pairing of these two scenes illuminate
> larger themes in Book I of *The Once and Future King*?

The ants that Wart encounters in T. H. White's *The Once and Future King* repeatedly show signs of belligerence and heartless efficiency. By contrast, the geese demonstrate the virtues of empathy and generosity. Like the ants and geese, several other opposed—or dichotomous—pairs that Wart encounters symbolize the conflict between might and right. By including the ants and geese in this assortment of dichotomies, White reinforces his idea that a large part of our education is choosing between a warlike and a compassionate way of life.

Wart's encounter with the ants teaches him that one way to live involves denying your spiritual needs, failing to recognize the individuality of the people around you, and investing all of your energy in a mindless, aggressive quest for survival. The ants have an impoverished, depressing language that strips them of the ability to communicate deeply and subtly: All adjectives are crowded into the categories "Done" and "Not Done." The one notable interaction between ants is a parody of fellowship; without speaking or acknowledging his partner, an ant sometimes gorges on the food stored in the partner's body. The ants have numbers, not names, referring to one executed worker as "310099/WD." Their unquestioning belief in the virtues of capital punishment and war suggests that they are intellectually inactive: There is no room for debate, no possibility of questioning whether all dissidents should immediately be killed. They mumble clichéd words of praise for the queen, but the only positive thing they can say about her is that she is belligerent. The ants do not demonstrate compassion, skepticism, or intellectual curiosity.

By contrast, the geese celebrate their sense of freedom, civic-mindedness, and tranquility. They show a genuine interest in one another, as, for example, Lyo-lyok gives Wart a name and engages him in an intellectual debate. Lyo-lyok's scorn for war indicates that she is interested in more creative, challenging ways of solving problems; she attributes Wart's interest in fighting to the fact that he is "a baby." The songs of the geese celebrate their freedom—"free, free," "wild and free"—and part of their creed is that there are no boundaries in the air. The image of flying and soaring contrasts starkly with the earthbound claustrophobia of the ants' colony. The geese take pride in their culture, support one another, and patiently consider opinions that differ from their own.

Like the ants and geese, several other potential role models for Wart force him to weigh "might" against "right." Because he is "a born follower," Wart admires the forceful boy Kay, whose petulance is evident in his haughty class distinctions and his attempt to claim the magical sword for himself. On the other hand, Merlyn, a vocal critic of Kay, encourages Wart to adopt a life of contemplation and to recognize that knightly battles are ridiculous. Wart wants to emulate rooks, who "mob their enemies," but he also listens to Merlyn and Archimedes when they point out that rooks are thoughtless, neglectful parents. Wart admires the foolish machismo of Mr. P. and the blustering combatants Sir Grummore and King Pellinore, but he also takes in the words of the badger, who praises the loving, public-spirited geese. Nearly everyone Wart encounters forces him to consider the competing virtues of compassion and aggression.

By making the ant/goose contrast a major theme of Wart's childhood, White suggests that each of us must choose between a covetous and a large-minded way of life. He does not imply that the choice is simple: Indeed, the abundance of foolish, belligerent characters in Book I leads us to believe that a life of compassion may be an impossible ideal. Instead of a sermon, *The Once and Future King* is a celebration of quests—a portrait of one flawed boy's attempt to live wisely. With his gentle sense of humor, White encourages us to examine the many sidesteps, failings, and instances of antlike behavior in our own lives.

GLOSSARY OF LITERARY TERMS

ANTAGONIST

The entity that acts to frustrate the goals of the *protagonist*. The antagonist is usually another *character* but may also be a non-human force.

ANTIHERO / ANTIHEROINE

A *protagonist* who is not admirable or who challenges notions of what should be considered admirable.

CHARACTER

A person, animal, or any other thing with a personality that appears in a *narrative*.

CLIMAX

The moment of greatest intensity in a text or the major turning point in the *plot*.

CONFLICT

The central struggle that moves the *plot* forward. The conflict can be the *protagonist*'s struggle against fate, nature, society, or another person.

FIRST-PERSON POINT OF VIEW

A literary style in which the *narrator* tells the story from his or her own *point of view* and refers to himself or herself as "I." The narrator may be an active participant in the story or just an observer.

HERO / HEROINE

The principal *character* in a literary work or *narrative*.

IMAGERY

Language that brings to mind sense-impressions, representing things that can be seen, smelled, heard, tasted, or touched.

MOTIF

A recurring idea, structure, contrast, or device that develops or informs the major *themes* of a work of literature.

NARRATIVE

A story.

LITERARY ANALYSIS

NARRATOR

The person (sometimes a *character*) who tells a story; the *voice* assumed by the writer. The narrator and the author of the work of literature are not the same person.

PLOT

The arrangement of the events in a story, including the sequence in which they are told, the relative emphasis they are given, and the causal connections between events.

POINT OF VIEW

The *perspective* that a *narrative* takes toward the events it describes.

PROTAGONIST

The main *character* around whom the story revolves.

SETTING

The location of a *narrative* in time and space. Setting creates mood or atmosphere.

SUBPLOT

A secondary *plot* that is of less importance to the overall story but may serve as a point of contrast or comparison to the main plot.

SYMBOL

An object, *character,* figure, or color that is used to represent an abstract idea or concept. Unlike an *emblem,* a symbol may have different meanings in different contexts.

SYNTAX

The way the words in a piece of writing are put together to form lines, phrases, or clauses; the basic structure of a piece of writing.

THEME

A fundamental and universal idea explored in a literary work.

TONE

The author's attitude toward the subject or *characters* of a story or poem or toward the reader.

VOICE

An author's individual way of using language to reflect his or her own personality and attitudes. An author communicates voice through *tone, diction,* and *syntax.*

LITERARY ANALYSIS

A Note on Plagiarism

Plagiarism—presenting someone else's work as your own—rears its ugly head in many forms. Many students know that copying text without citing it is unacceptable. But some don't realize that even if you're not quoting directly, but instead are paraphrasing or summarizing, *it is plagiarism* unless you cite the source.

Here are the most common forms of plagiarism:

- Using an author's phrases, sentences, or paragraphs without citing the source
- Paraphrasing an author's ideas without citing the source
- Passing off another student's work as your own

How do you steer clear of plagiarism? You should *always* acknowledge all words and ideas that aren't your own by using quotation marks around verbatim text or citations like footnotes and endnotes to note another writer's ideas. For more information on how to give credit when credit is due, ask your teacher for guidance or visit www.sparknotes.com.

REVIEW & RESOURCES

QUIZ

1. What is King Arthur's nickname as a child?

   A. Cully
   B. The Wart
   C. The Nose
   D. Kay

2. Who are Queen Morgause's children?

   A. Gawaine, Gareth, Mordred, and Guenever
   B. Agravaine, Gawaine, Gaheris, and Uther
   C. Agravaine, Gawaine, Gaheris, Gareth, and Mordred
   D. Gawaine, Gaheris, Lamorak, Mordred, and Lot

3. Where does King Arthur's final battle against King Lot take place?

   A. Camelot
   B. The Out Isles
   C. Orkney
   D. Bedegraine

4. At the end of Book II, what does the narrator say is the cause of Arthur's tragedy?

   A. He tried to murder his son, Mordred
   B. He killed an unarmed man
   C. He slept with his half-sister Morgause
   D. He committed adultery

5. Why did Sir Ector and not Arthur's birth father, Uther Pendragon, raise Arthur?

   A. Arthur was conceived out of wedlock
   B. Uther was too busy fighting the Gaels
   C. Uther didn't know that Arthur had been born
   D. Sir Ector kidnapped Arthur

6. Who is Mordred's closest ally?

    A. Gaheris
    B. Agravaine
    C. Arthur
    D. Gawaine

7. How does Gawaine die?

    A. He dies fighting his brother Gareth
    B. He dies of old age
    C. He dies fighting Mordred's forces in England
    D. He dies fighting Lancelot in France

8. Why does the Wart pull the sword out of the stone?

    A. He wants to be king of England
    B. He has left his own sword at the inn
    C. Merlyn tells him to pull the sword
    D. Kay has forgotten his sword at the inn

9. What is Lancelot's son named?

    A. Gaheris
    B. Lionel
    C. Ban
    D. Galahad

10. Why doesn't Lancelot find the Holy Grail?

    A. He is wounded in battle
    B. He is a sinner
    C. Galahad gets to it first
    D. He cannot find the Holy Grail

11. On what text is *The Once and Future King* based?

    A. *Sir Gawain and the Green Knight*
    B. Malory's *Morte d'Arthur*
    C. Descartes's *Discours de la Methode*
    D. Montaigne's *Essais*

12. Why do Arthur and Gawaine lay siege to Lancelot's castle in France?

   A. Because Lancelot is having an affair with Guenever
   B. Because Arthur wants to expand his kingdom
   C. Because Lancelot has kidnapped Guenever
   D. Because they think that Lancelot has killed Gareth and Gaheris

13. Why does Lancelot sleep with Elaine?

   A. Lancelot thinks she is Guenever
   B. Elaine promises not to tell anyone
   C. Lancelot wants to have a son
   D. Lancelot is under a spell

14. What is the name of Merlyn's owl?

   A. Degalis
   B. Archie
   C. Archimedes
   D. Troy

15. While living with Elaine, Lancelot disguises himself and goes by which of the following names?

   A. Le Chevalier Noir
   B. Le Chevalier Mal Fet
   C. Sir Galahad
   D. The Wild Man

16. Why does Agravaine kill his mother, Morgause?

   A. She has disowned him
   B. She whipped him as a child
   C. She is having an affair with Sir Aglovale
   D. She is having an affair with Sir Lamorak

17. Which animal does Merlyn turn the Wart into first?

   A. A badger
   B. A perch
   C. A hawk
   D. An ant

18. What is the name of the hawk that the Wart follows in the woods?

    A. Sir Ector
    B. Hob
    C. Cully
    D. Kay

19. Why do Sir Palomides and Sir Grummore disguise themselves as the Questing Beast?

    A. To cheer up King Pellinore
    B. To frighten Queen Morgause
    C. To entertain themselves
    D. To seduce the real Questing Beast

20. What is the one thing that Merlyn forgets to warn Arthur about in time?

    A. That Mordred will betray him
    B. That Lancelot will have an affair with Guenever
    C. That Lancelot will betray him
    D. That Arthur is Morgause's half-brother

21. Why does Lancelot battle Sir Turquine?

    A. Because Sir Turquine wants revenge for his brother's death
    B. Because Sir Turquine is defending the Holy Grail
    C. To rescue his cousin, Sir Lionel
    D. To rescue Agravaine

22. Who is the only person to defeat Lancelot in single combat?

    A. Arthur
    B. Galahad
    C. Gawaine
    D. Tristram

23. What are King Arthur's allies in France named?

    A. Bors and Kay
    B. Gawaine and Gaheris
    C. Ban and Bors
    D. Pierre and François

24. Why is Arthur's table round?

    A. To prevent jealousy and competition among the knights
    B. To allow every knight a good view of King Arthur, who sits in the middle
    C. To use timber, a limited resource in Camelot, more efficiently
    D. To symbolize the unity of King Arthur's kingdom

25. Who is King Arthur's real father?

    A. King Pellinore
    B. Sir Ector
    C. Uther Pendragon
    D. Merlyn

REVIEW & RESOURCES

ANSWER KEY

1: B; 2: C; 3: D; 4: C; 5: A; 6: B; 7: C; 8: D; 9: D; 10: B; 11: B; 12: D;
13: A; 14: C; 15: B; 16: D; 17: B; 18: C; 19: C; 20: D; 21: C; 22: B;
23: C; 24: A; 25: C

Suggestions for Further Reading

ASHE, GEOFFREY. *The Discovery of King Arthur.* New York: Henry Holt, 1987.

BREWER, ELIZABETH. *T.H. White's* THE ONCE AND FUTURE KING. Suffolk and Rochester: D.S. Brewer, 1993.

CRANE, J. K. *T. H. White.* New York: Twayne Publishers, 1974.

MALORY, SIR THOMAS. *Le Morte Darthur.* (Norton Critical Edition). STEPHEN H.A. SHEPHERD, ed. New York: W.W. Norton, 2003.

SNYDER, CHRISTOPHER. *The World of King Arthur.* London: Thames and Hudson, 2000.

TENNYSON, ALFRED. *Idylls of the King.* New York: Penguin, 1989.

WARNER, S. T. *T. H. White.* London: Jonathan Cape, 1967.

WHITE, T. H. *The Book of Merlyn: The Unpublished Conclusion to The Once and Future King.* Austin: University of Texas Press, 1977.